COPING WITH YOUR DIFFICULT OLDER PARENT

Coping with Your Difficult Older Parent

A Guide for Stressed-Out Children

Grace Lebow & Barbara Kane
with Irwin Lebow

HARPER

NEW YORK • LONDON • TORONTO • SYDNEY

HarperCollins books may be purchased for educational, business, or sales promotional use. For information, please e-mail the Special Markets Department at SPsales@harpercollins.com.

First Avon Books edition published 1999.

Reprinted in Quill 2002.

Designed by Kellan Peck

Library of Congress Cataloging-in-Publication Data
Lebow, Grace.
    Coping with your difficult older parent : a guide for stressed-out children / Grace Lebow & Barbara Kane, with Irwin Lebow.
        p.   cm.
      1. Aging parents—United States—Family relationships. 2. Aging parents—Care—United States. 3. Adult children—United States—Psychology. 4. Adult children—United States—Family relationships. 5. Communication in the family—United States. 6. Adjustment (Psychology) in old age—United States. I. Kane, Barbara, 1949-II. Lebow, Irwin. I I. Title.
HQ1064.U5L42   1999   98-47289
306.874—dc21   CIP

ISBN 0-380-79750-X

15 16 17 18 19 RRD 30 29

◆

To your difficult parents—
may their pain be better understood.

Preface

◆

In 1982 the two of us established Aging Network Services (http://www.AgingNetS.com), a social work care management agency dedicated to helping older people and their families. It did not take long for us to recognize that well over half the adult children (we call them *grownchildren*) who came to us for psychotherapy were in a state of stress over their "difficult" parents. They used the word "difficult," not so much because of the physical burden of caring for parents in a state of decline, but because of the emotional drain of trying to help parents who were hard to help. In many instances the child had distanced himself from his parents either geographically or emotionally. But now that the parent was suffering from the ravages of old age, the child was forced to step in to help and confront anew the parent he could no longer escape. In the intervening years we have helped many hundreds of such clients with their difficult parents.

Grace also gained the perspective of a family member of a difficult parent when she and her husband Irwin took care of his mother in her later years. Indeed it was this experience that gave us the idea of writing a book that would share our experience with a much larger group of people. We tried out our ideas on professional colleagues as well as on laymen and received the universally enthusiastic response that a book like this was sorely needed.

The book fills a gap in the literature on eldercare. While there are many excellent books on eldercare in general, none address the parent with difficult behaviors to any significant extent. There are so many books on problem personalities, most of which are by therapists concerned with *treating* people with these difficulties, not with *helping others* cope with their behaviors. What's more, this literature hardly mentions the older population since older people with difficult personalities rarely seek therapy.

The book is filled with examples mostly taken from our practice. We asked about fifty clients to fill out the Difficult Parent Questionnaire at the beginning of the book as a trial balloon and then interviewed them to obtain a more in-depth understanding of the parent's personality and of the dynamics between parent and child. We are very grateful to these people who participated in the interviews, giving us their time and emotional energy. Of course, the stories in the book and the names of the protagonists were all changed to preserve anonymity. We wish we could thank them all here by name, but the same anonymity precludes us from doing this.

One person whom we are delighted to thank by name is Mary Dluhy, who was gracious enough to review our manuscript for technical accuracy. Mary, a highly respected clinician, is the prime mover in the effort to establish the Clinical Social Work Institute, a graduate school for clinical social workers.

A final note is in explanation of the way the book refers to counseling sessions with our clients. To avoid using the awkward term "the counselor" or, in a book with two authors, the confusing "I," we used the first person plural, "we," even though a client coming to Aging Network Services for help sees one of us, not both.

Grace Lebow and Barbara Kane
Bethesda, Maryland

Contents

◆

ix

COPING WITH YOUR DIFFICULT OLDER PARENT

Introduction

◆

"I cringe every time the phone rings in fear that it's Mom criticizing me for something else."

"I can never get away on vacation. Just when I am about to leave, my mother always gets sick and I have to stay home."

"I don't know what to do with my mom. She runs from doctor to doctor looking for a magic cure and ends up with no-good care."

"My father hasn't a clue as to how I think or feel about anything. It's his opinion that counts. He assumes that I think as he does."

"Yesterday, I was the best son in the world. I could do no wrong, and today I am 'heartless.' I can't even figure out what I did to deserve such treatment."

"My parents say they don't want to be a burden, yet they adamantly refuse all my suggestions. They only want me."

◆

These are typical of the statements we hear from clients every day. If you identify with any of them, chances are you are at your wit's end, perhaps even desperate. You are trying to do the best you can for your parent, yet all you succeed in doing is making yourself miserable. You may even use the word "difficult" to describe your parent's personality.

The statements are representative of only six of forty behaviors that we have identified as "difficult" and cataloged into a "Difficult Parent Questionnaire." Whenever children come

1

to see us for the first time and describe their parent as difficult, we show them the questionnaire and give them a few minutes to fill it out. As they go through the behaviors, these clients are often amazed to see how well their parents' behaviors match those in the questionnaire. Some are surprised and often relieved to discover there are many other parents just as difficult as or even more difficult than their own parents. They are even more relieved when we tell them there are things they can do to help both themselves and their parents.

Why don't you take just a few minutes to fill out the questionnaire for yourself?

DIFFICULT PARENT QUESTIONNAIRE
◆

The following questionnaire enables you to make an initial judgment of your parent's relative level of "difficulty." It contains forty problem behaviors in six categories. Check off each behavior that applies to your parent and add up the check marks.

A. Dependency Behaviors

Your parent:

_____ cannot tolerate being alone; wants you all the time.

_____ becomes physically ill or overtly hostile when confronted with separation.

_____ makes unreasonable and irrational demands upon their grownchildren and others.

_____ attaches himself or herself to another person (e.g., a daughter), leaning on that person for help with everything.

_____ is unable to make decisions or take responsibility for decisions, looking to their grownchildren and others for even trivial decisions.

_____ cannot allow himself or herself to depend on others even when you know he or she needs help.

B. "Turnoff" Behaviors

Your parent:

_____ tends to view others as all good or all bad. Sometimes the same person can be all good one day and all bad the next.

_____ is extremely negative and complains of unhappiness.

_____ is hypercritical of others and hypersensitive to criticism or blame.

_____ is tactless.

_____ has to be "right" all the time.

_____ is angry and hostile, while blaming others for the same characteristics.

_____ has temper tantrums, e.g., throws things, or uses abusive language.

_____ is distrustful and suspicious, sometimes to the point of paranoia.

_____ pushes people away, or even cuts off the relationship.

C. Self-centered Behaviors

Your Parent:

_____ has a distorted self-image, viewing self as "something special" at one end, or inadequate at the other.

_____ interprets events solely as to how they affect him or her, oblivious to the effect on others.

_____ is insensitive to the needs of others while, at the same time, thinks of self as generous.

_____ guards his or her own turf.

_____ is jealous of others.

D. Controlling Behaviors

Your parent:

_____ manipulates others by the use of such techniques as guilt and flattery.

_____ is passive-aggressive, i.e., antagonizes others by behaving passively, e.g., by procrastinating or withdrawing or by other means.

_____ elicits feelings in others that reflect his or her own feelings such as helplessness or rage.

_____ cannot tolerate differences in things pertaining to life-style, ranging from the mundane (eating, dressing) to important values (rearing children).

_____ becomes angry and hostile when the persons they are trying to control don't behave as desired. i.e., don't "heel."

_____ makes demands so excessive that the opposite is achieved.

E. Self-destructive Behaviors

Your parent:

_____ has ever been addicted to alcohol, drugs, or medicine.

_____ has ever had eating disorders, e.g., overeating or refusal to eat.

_____ has ever behaved compulsively, such as by gambling, hair-pulling, excessive washing, etc.

_____ has ever been accident-prone.

_____ behaves masochistically, e.g., doesn't comply with dietary restrictions or refuses to take medication.

_____ has ever been suicidal or threatened suicide.

F. Fearfulness Behaviors

Your parent:

_____ is a worrywart, anxious over real or imagined occurrences.

_____ is subject to panic attacks.

_____ has phobias, such as fear of crowds, germs, etc.

_____ has sleeping problems.

_____ behaves ritualistically and superstitiously.

_____ has magical expectations, e.g., goes doctor shopping to look for a cure.

_____ tends to deny the obvious, e.g., symptoms of illness.

_____ is preoccupied with physical problems, real or imagined.

_____*Total*

If your score is ten or less, your parent is slightly diffi-cult; if between eleven and twenty, moderately difficult; and twenty-one or above, very difficult.

So Your Parent Is Difficult

We hope you have gone through the questionnaire and tallied your parent's score. If you skipped over it, we suggest you go back and fill it out. The questionnaire gives you a way of comparing your parent's behavior with the whole scope of problem behaviors. Moreover, the book's organization is based on the six categories in the questionnaire, and identifying where your parent's behaviors fit in to the categories will help you get the most out of the book.

Our aim in writing the book is to give you practical tips on dealing with your difficult parent. The book is a distillation of more than twenty-five years of experience we each have as social workers helping older people and their families. Our work covers the gamut of activities from counseling older people and their children to *care management:* for example, helping older people obtain practical services such as home care and assisting the family in making such life decisions as whether to move and, if so, where.

At least one-half of the *grownchildren* (we prefer this term to *adult children*) who come to us consider their parents to be difficult. It is easy to understand why this proportion is so high. If your parent is easy to get along with, you may be able to help her by yourself, even when the problems are difficult and the situations stressful. But when the older person's behaviors match those in the questionnaire, perhaps driving you to the point of desperation, you are more likely to seek out professional help. It is our experience with many hundreds of such older people that enabled us to compile the list of diffi-cult behaviors in the questionnaire.

Most of these older people are described by their grown-children as having been difficult as long as they can remember. The relationship between parent and child has therefore been colored by these personality traits throughout the child's life-time. A grownchild who may have overlooked, ignored, or distanced himself from his parent in the past is forced into more frequent contact when his parent is older and needs help. He discovers that the problem behaviors have not disappeared, that the illnesses and losses of later life have made them even worse, and that his own past emotional baggage is still alive and readily activated.

◆

Most difficult parents have been difficult all their lives.

Difficult behaviors can also show up for the first time later in life after your parent suffers an illness, a loss, or some other traumatic event. Under these circumstances you can realistically hope the difficult behaviors will subside with the right treatment or even disappear in time—something that does not often happen when the difficult behaviors are lifelong. Of course there are exceptions to this rule. The most important of these is when the cause is the onset of a chronic disease that impairs brain functioning, such as Alzheimer's disease or a major stroke. In such situations, the person necessarily behaves differently from before, although even here there are simple things you can do to manage the behavioral changes (Alzheimer's disease and related disorders are not the focus of this book. The Bibliography at the end of the book contains several excellent references on this subject.)

◆

When difficult behaviors appear later in life, there is hope the behaviors will disappear.

This book summarizes our many years of experience with helping grownchildren and others in dealing with difficult older people. It will help you respond to your parent's difficult behaviors, even if you are convinced that nothing can help because "no one can possibly be as difficult as *my* mother." Our hope is that the variety of examples presented in this book will stimulate new insights that you can apply to your own particular situation with your parent.

HOW TO GET OUT OF A PARALYZING RUT WITH YOUR PARENTS

You are at your wit's end. You think your parent is so

difficult that improving your relationship is hopeless. But don't despair—in almost every instance, there is something *you* can do to improve the situation for both of you. After all, wasn't this your hope when you bought this book?

The first step is to recognize as a responsible grownchild that the problem is a mutual one. If you focus solely on your parent's problem behaviors and not the relationship between the two of you, chances are you will get nowhere. A difficult person doesn't even realize how others perceive her. It may well look to her as if you and everyone else have the problem.

♦

The problem is a mutual one.

Then again, even if your parent recognizes her own personality problems, which of you is more likely to want to change or, more importantly, who has the greatest capacity to change? The answer is, of course, you, particularly if your parent has been difficult all her life.

♦

You have more capacity to change than your parent.

One of the things this book will do for you is give you fresh ideas about what to do about your painful relationship with your parent. Grownchildren come to see us because they feel stuck in a rut with a difficult parent. No matter how hard they try, no matter what they do, nothing ever seems to change. Their difficult parents aggravate them, and they always react the same way and get the same negative response. You will see many such no-win situations as you go through the book.

♦

Changing means getting out of your old rut and trying something different.

Getting out of the rut means making a fundamental change in your assumptions about what is wrong with your relationship with your parent and in the steps you take to improve it. Perhaps you are the perpetual optimist trying to get your parent to change her ways, convinced that if she does she will love you more and you will love her more. Or perhaps you are the perpetual defeatist, who recognizes that there is little hope of your parent changing and resigns yourself to acting exactly as your parent wants you to act or else cutting off your relationship.

This book will show you ways of getting out of these and similar paralyzing situations. You may not even be aware of how stuck you are. If so, this book will help you gain this recognition. It will help you understand your parent's difficulties and be more accepting of her limitations. And with this understanding you will be able to feel more compassion for your parent and, at the same time, be able to live your own life without being at the mercy of her behaviors. But keep in mind that achieving this objective doesn't happen overnight. It takes time, hard work, and patience, just like any other personal goal worth reaching.

One of our clients is now able to say, "I used to think that something was wrong with me because I didn't love my mother like my friends loved their mothers. But I have come to understand that my mother has been difficult to get along with all her life. She finds fault with everyone, including me. Nothing is ever right. Although I don't love her more, even with this new understanding, I do accept her as my mom with a lot of shortcomings."

◆

Understanding keeps
your buttons from
getting pushed.

As you go through this book you will see examples in which grownchildren are able to ascribe their parent's difficult behaviors to certain events in their backgrounds. Such understanding is always helpful in getting grownchildren to change the way they deal with their parents. However, we have found that the most important thing for grownchildren to understand is that *something* is causing their parent's difficult behaviors, even if they don't know exactly what that something is. Coming to terms with this helps you recognize that your parent is not acting in difficult ways either capriciously or deliberately, but rather because she cannot help it. She may be a tortured person suffering from a personality that allows her no peace with herself. Perhaps she has felt this way all her life and has managed to survive the vicissitudes of life in one way or another. Now in older age, with the added physical and emotional problems that everyone feels in the aging process, she is even more burdened with herself and her personality.

Once you recognize these things about your own difficult parent, you will come to see her in a different light. You will be less angry and more empathetic. You will learn to rechannel your energies from the fruitless task of trying to get her to change to the more productive goal of learning practical ways of coping with her as she is. This is the way we have helped our clients, and this is what we hope this book can do for you.

HOW TO USE THE BOOK

The book contains nine chapters and a brief Appendix. In the first seven chapters, we go through the difficult behaviors in the questionnaire in a systematic way, devoting one chapter to each of the behavior categories—except for the large "turn-off" category, to which we devote two chapters. In each of these chapters we present a number of examples taken from our caseloads—of course, the situations are altered and all the names are fictitious. From these examples we give you practical tips for dealing with the particular behaviors. We have found from experience that role-playing is one of the most effective ways in which grownchildren can practice new ways of communicating with their parents, and we present many role-plays in illustrating our suggestions. These cases illustrate people who have been difficult all their lives as well as those who developed later-life difficult behaviors.

You can start out, if you choose, with the chapters relating to the behavioral categories that most apply to your parent. Thus, if your mother's fearfulness is your major concern, you will probably not be able to keep yourself from going right to Chapter 7. But since each chapter builds on the preceding one, we suggest you go back to the beginning and read the earlier chapters also. The six categories of difficult behaviors are so related that you will learn more about your parent's particular behaviors in the context of the others.

The last two chapters depart from the questionnaire to address two issues crucial to both older people and their grownchildren. The first of these issues, discussed in Chapter

8, is the process of dealing with the losses that are inherent to the aging process. People with difficult personalities have a harder time doing this than others, and the way they react to loss often perplexes their children.

The concluding chapter, entitled "How to Keep from Being Difficult Yourself," addresses the fears of many grown-children that they will be as difficult to get along with as their difficult parents. Its message is that even if you see a little of your difficult mother in yourself, it is within your control to keep this from happening.

The Appendix is an overview of the various theories that attempt to explain the source of difficult behaviors in older adults.

The book concludes with a Bibliography on the theoretical aspects of behavioral difficulties and practical topics in eldercare.

1

WHEN YOUR PARENT CLINGS TO YOU

DEPENDENCY BEHAVIORS

When your parent:

◆ cannot tolerate being alone; wants you all the time.

◆ becomes physically ill or overtly hostile when confronted with separation.

◆ makes unreasonable and irrational demands upon their grownchildren and others.

◆ attaches himself or herself to another person (e.g., a daughter), leaning on that person for help with everything.

◆ is unable to make decisions or take responsibility for decisions, looking to their grownchildren and others for even trivial decisions.

◆ cannot allow himself or herself to depend on others even when you know he or she needs help

---

A DEPENDENT MOTHER
◆

Al dialed the phone with trepidation. He was at a public phone in the theater lobby. The curtain was to go up in just a few minutes. He and his wife had just rushed into the theater after grabbing a quick dinner at a restaurant a few steps away. But before taking their seats for an evening of relaxation, Al knew if he did not call his mother, there would be hell to pay. He always called on the nights he did not visit her. The problem this evening was that his call was about one-half hour after the customary time.

He was not sure how she would react. Sometimes she would not notice if the call was a little later than expected.

There were even those rare occasions on which she noticed but did not rub it in. But this was not to be one of those nights. As soon as he answered her hello with a cheery "Hello, Mother," he was greeted by a cold, angry voice saying, "Where were you? I have been trying to get you all night."

"I'm at the theater, Mom. Miriam and I both had to work late this evening and we barely had enough time for supper. I have to be in my seat in just a couple of minutes and I wanted to call first to see how you are today."

"I'm just fine," came the hard and steely reply. These words were followed by a sharp click. "Can you beat that? She hung up on me," he said to Miriam as he came out of the telephone booth. "I hope you're not surprised," she said as they were taking their seats. He was indeed not surprised. Things like this had happened often enough for him not to take it so personally. Yet, no matter how often it happened and how much he tried to accept it nonchalantly, he still felt the pain. All during the evening his mind would wander from the stage before him to that telephone call. He kept wondering what he could have said or done differently to avoid this upsetting exchange. Al had learned by bitter experience to try to call each evening early enough to avoid these unpleasant interactions. Moreover, he also had learned to visit in person two to three times a week to appease his guilt and try to keep his mother happy.

Of course, the word "happy" is a relative one. The fact was that Bea, Al's eighty-eight-year-old mother, was chronically unhappy. She had been a complainer as long as Al could remember, and the complaints had only worsened as she grew older and began to suffer some of the physical impairments of older age. Despite this, she had gotten by reasonably well during most of her married life with a devoted husband, good children, and financial security. Now with her husband gone and her health not what it used to be, she had all the more reason to feel unhappy.

The basic problem, as Al saw it, was that his mother was such a dependent person. All her life, she had leaned upon her husband. She had no friends of her own. She didn't be-

long to a bridge club or play mah-jongg, as did other women in the neighborhood. One of Al's earliest recollections was the way in which she would wait anxiously for his father to come home at night. Night after night, year after year, he would come through the door at seven o'clock sharp, and night after night, year after year, Bea would greet him with, "Where were you? Why can't you come home earlier?"

And this dependence only increased as the years passed. And now that her husband was dead, she expected her son to be at her beck and call. It's not that Al minded taking care of things for her. But it was unreasonable, he thought, to be unable to go to the theater without feeling her watchful eye. What could he do to cope better?

◆

A Professional Can Help Get You out of a Rut with Your Difficult Parent

Al and Miriam had found that dealing with Bea had been difficult for some time and was becoming more so. They had been coping with the situation by doing as Bea wanted and avoiding doing those things that irritated her. They visited her regularly every Monday and Thursday. Every Sunday they brought her over to their home for dinner. They remembered every occasion. In short, they behaved pretty much as she wanted them to behave. While this pampering didn't satisfy her enough to assuage her ever-present anger, it held it reasonably in check.

Sometimes they would lose their tempers and argue with her when she took out her venom on her housekeeper or on someone else in the family. Then she would get even angrier with them for taking "their side." But she would get over it after a few days, and things would return to their usual state. Al was becoming increasingly angry at having to walk on eggshells all the time. Would she behave better if he gave her hell the next day, told her that he was insulted, and made her apologize? Maybe she needed to be held to account. Al was confused as to what tack to take. It was the theater incident that convinced him he couldn't go on this way and pushed him to seek counseling.

◆

Getting help is important. See a counselor or join a support group. It helps to recognize that many others have the same problems as you.

Al's story is typical of the ones we hear every day in our practice when grownchildren come to seek ways of dealing with parents who are difficult to get along with. One of the first things Al learned was there are lots of people in his position and each believes no one else in the world can possibly have a parent as difficult as his own. Sometimes simply recognizing there are many others in the same boat is of some comfort to a grownchild.

Al and Miriam also learned specific dos and don'ts for handling their problems. When you read over these tips it is easy to see how many of them are applicable not just to Al but to many people in other situations similar to his. If your parent is at all like Bea, these tips will give you fresh ideas about how you can cope.

Changing the Way You React to Your Parent

◆

Don't get angry and give your parent hell. It makes both of you feel worse and solves nothing.

Al and Miriam were doing certain things instinctively, as others in similar situations often do, and these things were not working for them. For example: They were getting angry, losing their tempers, and bawling out Al's mother. No matter how exasperated you become with your difficult parent, anger doesn't solve anything. It only makes you and your parent feel worse. Your parent can't see her own shortcomings and will only see that her son has a short fuse. Even if you hold her to account and make her apologize, she won't understand and won't learn from the experience.

Another thing Al and Miriam were doing was arguing and trying to reason with Bea. This conversation between Al and his mother on the day after the theater incident illustrates how nonproductive reasoning can be in circumstances such as these.

AL: Mom, you want me to call you every night. But some nights I do go out. Like last night I was at the theater with Miriam. But I wanted to say hello to keep you from worrying, so I called you from the theater.

BEA: I was frantic when you didn't call by six o'clock. You have time to do everything but call your mother.

AL: [*beginning to lose his cool*] So if I don't call exactly when you want me to, you worry. You have to understand that I can't call you precisely when you want all the time.

BEA: [*says nothing, but stares coldly*]

AL: [*getting angrier by the minute*] You are the most unreasonable, demanding person I have ever known. I can't do exactly as you want all the time. Let's face it. If you can't change your attitude, you'll just have to worry sometimes.

Isn't it interesting that Al's reaction to his mother's response when he called her from the theater was similar to her response to him? He felt rejected, cut off, and furious. And then he told her what to do just as she always told him what to do when his actions were not to her liking. If your parent is anything like Bea, you know that it's hard to avoid feeling this way. But try not to let yourself behave in the way your parent does.

◆

Take care not to follow in your mother's footsteps.

Feeling furious at his mother all the time, it was only natural for Al to play the blame game. Usually the blame was directed at his mother. It was all her fault for holding him on a tight leash and behaving in so many other unreasonable ways. But often in his cooler

◆

Don't blame yourself or your parent. Trying to find a scapegoat only makes things worse.

moments, Al would turn the blame on himself. His mother doesn't behave so irrationally with many other people. Maybe it's something that he is doing.

◆

Don't try to reason with your parent. Her behavior is not rational.

During these cooler moments, Al tried to reason with his mother to get her to change her behavior, even though it never worked. But it is just not realistic to expect someone like Bea to change a lifetime of dependent behavior. If Al is to feel better, he has to work the other side of the problem, that is, see how he can modify the way *he* reacts toward his mother.

◆

Decide ahead of time what you can and cannot do.

We explained to Al that for his long-term peace of mind, he couldn't keep doing everything his mother wanted him to do to keep her from getting angry. We told him that he had to decide what *he* thought *he* could reasonably do and stick to it. The same is true for you. If your mother is pressuring you to visit her more often than you think is necessary or desirable, decide how often you can do it comfortably. If she calls you more often than you would like, get an answering machine to take some of the calls. Your mother will not like your limits at first. She may never get used to them and may keep complaining. But stick to them anyway. They are your boundaries. For your own well-being you have to be firm about what is best for you. This is the way you can preserve your relationship with your parent.

Sometimes it takes a crutch of some kind to help you change your mode of interaction with your parent. For example, we suggested that Al make a calendar chart for himself specifying when he will visit and call his mother each week. "Discuss it with Miriam and then put the chart on the refrigerator door to serve as a reminder and a commitment for both of you," we recommended.

Al followed his counselor's advice and succeeded in limiting his contacts with his mother. It wasn't easy, but it was worth the effort. Here is one of the phone conversations he had with his mother after digesting what the counselor had to say. Note that he doesn't rationalize, argue, or blame himself or her.

AL: Hi, Mother. How are you doing today?

BEA: How should I be doing? What do you expect? I'm nervous and worried and sitting here waiting for my devoted [*said with sarcasm*] son to come see me.

AL: [*Normally he would be triggered to respond with irritation, but now he changes the subject.*] You'll get a kick out of the picture your granddaughter did in school the other day. I brought it here to show you.

BEA: That's cute. It's been so long since I've seen her. I miss her. It's about time you brought her over to see me.

AL: We'll all be here this Sunday. Remember that is our day together. We'll bring the brunch.

BEA: Oh, yes. All I rate is one day a week.

AL: I'll look forward to Sunday, Mother. Bye.

Note how Bea's insecurity and dependency come out in each of her responses to her son's comments and questions. Before Al's sessions with us, such responses would have triggered an irritable reaction in him, and then mother and son would have been off and running. But now Al has taken a different tack. He has limited his face-to-face interactions to one per week, and in his intermediate phone calls he has adopted a new attitude. He responds positively to his mother's complaints. He says what he can do, not what he cannot do, and he doesn't feel guilty about it. Most importantly, Al is now able to empathize with his mother's underlying feelings of misery rather than addressing the content of the issues between them.

Of course, Al did not change overnight. He had to work at it before he could feel comfortable with this new approach. At first it caused even more stress, but it was well worth it in the end.

Pay attention to your own physical and mental well-being. You won't be of any use to yourself or your parent if

◆

Be flexible.

Take care of yourself.

Try stress-reducing tactics.

Humor is one of the best.

your health suffers. Take vacations. Try using humor or any other stress-reducing technique that helps you. Dan Greenburg wrote a very insightful little book over thirty years ago called *How to Be a Jewish Mother,* in which he pokes fun at the traditional overprotective, guilt-inducing mother. Greenburg invokes what he calls the "Jewish Mother's Cardinal Rule: Let your child hear you sigh every day; if *you* don't know what he's done to make you suffer, *he* will." Try bringing humor into the situation. It just might help.

♦

Recognize that deep down your parent feels miserable.
These feelings are what are at the root of difficult behaviors.

The most important thing the counselor explained to Al is what drives people such as his mother and the many other people like her. Her difficult behaviors are the result of miserable feelings about herself that she has had to bear all her life. For better or worse, she is stuck with those feelings; they are part of her personality. The difficult behaviors are the automatic way in which she places these feelings on others. It may seem that she should know better—she is a smart lady. But her behavior is irrational and has nothing to do with intelligence. At the heart of Al's new attitude was his coming to grips with this insight.

Once you understand something about your mother's personality and how she got that way, you can then shift from frustration and hurt—as Al did—to tolerance and compassion for her inner torments. You will now be in a better position to find ways of dealing with her that will reduce your own stress along with hers. As a way of arriving at this understanding, it is helpful to a grownchild such as Al to find out all he can of his mother's early life from stories that his mother and others in the family may have told him. One client put it this way: "Understanding my mother helps not to hate her." Another client was even able to reach the point of saying, "Understanding my mother helped me love her more."

Here is another example of a mother whose personality is very similar to Bea's. She is just as difficult as Bea to deal with, but for different reasons.

THE MOTHER WHO GETS SICK WHEN HER SON GOES AWAY

◆

"I'm so sick. I'm so sick. I have one of my bad headaches again. When are you coming over? It's so lonely here."

"I'll be over a little later this afternoon, Mother. I'll get the nurse to look in on you."

It was as if her son, Morton, had said nothing. "I'm so sick," was the continued reply, repeated again and again like a broken record.

Rose, Morton's mother, is living nearby in a retirement residence. She was widowed more than fifteen years ago. Joe's death had been a hard blow. In all these years she had never really come to terms with it. Her world, which had never been a particularly sunny place, was cast into a gloom that never seemed to lift. Nevertheless, she somehow managed to live alone and get along. Her only friends were Joe's sisters. She lived near them, saw them often, and spoke to them every day, often many times. But as the years passed, two of them had died, and the third taken terminally ill. Rose, too, was in declining health. She walked with the greatest of difficulty. Her stomach was chronically upset. Her eyes continually teared since a cataract operation. Then there were all the other illnesses about which she complained constantly.

At the time of her husband's death, her only son, Morton, and his wife, Greta, lived a thousand miles away. Yet, despite the distance, they kept close tabs on her, visiting her a few times a year and inviting her to spend time with them at their home. They took care of her finances and pacified her landlord, whom she was constantly haranguing with her incessant demands and complaints. Finally, they came to the realization that Rose no longer could make it on her own. After many visits and painful conversations they were able to convince her that living alone was no longer feasible; that it would be best if she would give up her apartment, pick up stakes, and move to their city.

But where should she live? They knew she really wanted

to move in with them. She hinted at it in so many ways, although she never said it directly. But they knew this was a recipe for disaster. It would never make her happy; nothing could. And it would make their lives miserable. They spoke to her about it, finally convincing her that, as much as they would like to have her move in with them, it wouldn't work since all the bedrooms were on the second floor, and she would have great difficulty negotiating the stairs. The fact that this business about the stairs was true didn't make them feel any better. They felt like a pair of hypocrites knowing very well that the stairs saved them from having to tell her the real reason. Finally, they persuaded her to move into a nearby retirement residence where most of her basic physical needs would be tended to.

Although the point about the stairs was irrefutable and she knew it, nevertheless she would mutter to her nurse's aide that her son and "witch" of a daughter-in-law didn't want her around. She never should have left her former home, she said, and blamed them for "forcing" her to do so. She felt lonesome at the retirement residence. All her fellow residents were cold and unfriendly. The spells of stomach trouble came with increasing frequency and severity. Headaches began to occur, also with increasing frequency. At the first sign of a symptom, she would call her son rather than the nurse on duty at the residence. She had so many complaints that it was not easy to distinguish imaginary symptoms from real ones. Morton felt angry that his mother was manipulating him with her imaginary illnesses. Then he felt guilty when he realized she was in real pain.

This latest call came at eleven o'clock on a Sunday morning. In just two hours they would be heading to the airport, the beginning of a week's vacation in the Caribbean. Morton called the nurses' station at the retirement residence and asked the nurse to look in on his mother to see what today's complaint was. But no sooner had he returned to his packing when the phone rang with a continuation of the broken record.

"Mother, the nurse is on her way up to see you. I'm sure

*she can give you something that will make you feel better.
I'll call you every day we are away. I'm sure you'll be fine."*
  The only reply was, "I'm so sick. I'm so sick."

◆

Did This Son Get Away?

How did the story end? Did Morton get away on that vacation?
Or did his mother's illness get to him and make him feel forced
to cancel his plans? As you can imagine, this was not the first
time this situation had presented itself. Sometimes Morton and
Greta left town feeling terribly guilty. Sometimes they canceled
their plans and then felt angry and miserable. This was one of
those times. But this time they were sufficiently upset with
Rose and themselves that they decided to come for some help.

Morton explained that they felt increasingly frustrated and
angry that his mother seemed to get sick whenever they were
about to go away, that the illnesses miraculously disappeared
when they decided not to go away. They concluded she was
faking. One of the many approaches they had tried was to give
her more and more preparation time to come to terms with
their leaving, but that only made it worse: She would get sicker
and sicker for a longer and longer time.

During the counseling sessions, Morton realized that getting sick had always been his mother's way of reacting to
stress. For example, when she was in her sixties, her cataract
operation had left her with a severe depression along with
uncontrolled rage directed toward the surgeon for what she
considered price gouging. Her eyes continued to tear for years
thereafter, as she went around muttering, "Six hundred dollars
an eye." Her husband was at his wit's end trying to pacify her.

Rose's life history indicated that deep down Rose was suffering from the same basic dependency problem as Bea. Therefore they were able to benefit from suggestions similar to those
that helped Al and his wife.

Are Rose's Illnesses for Real?

You can readily see that Rose and Bea are cut from the same cloth. Only the details are different. Your parent may also be similar to either or both of these women, and you may be reacting much as their sons do. Let's take the tips we gave Bea's children and see how they apply to Rose. This will help you with your own situation.

The no-win blame game. It would be easy for Morton to get angry and blame his mother for spoiling his vacations or blame himself for letting her get away with it. As we said before, don't fall into this no-win blame-game trap. It doesn't work.

You have to take care of your own needs. Of course, Morton knows that he has to get away on vacation every once in a while. The question is how to do it without taking it out on himself and his mother.

There is no substitute for understanding. As we indicated earlier, the only effective way to improve the situation is to come to terms with your parent's behavior and change the way you behave toward her. The first step is to understand something about why she behaves as she does. This is so fundamental that we repeat it here and throughout the book. It is the key for Morton to solve his vacation problem and for you to solve similar problems.

And that is where counseling can be helpful to you as it was for Morton and his wife. We helped them understand what was going on inside his mother—how frightened she was all the time, how she had to be constantly assured that her son was there to come to her aid.

Understanding that her dependent personality was at the root of her problems made it clear to Morton that doing such things as advising her to get involved in more activities or to be friendlier to the people in the retirement home was not going to work. In Rose's mind, only her son and not other people can calm her fears.

Therefore Morton had to be supporting and encouraging, to let his mother know that he understood how lonely she was. He had to be sympathetic, to tell her that he understood how difficult it must have been for her to get used to a new home and a new city at the same time, and to express the hope that she would make an adjustment and feel more like socializing with others as time goes on.

Of course, the thing that drove Morton up the wall was the way his reactions to his mother's illnesses kept him on a tight leash, interfered with his daily life, and prevented him from going away on vacation. We helped him understand that she wasn't *pretending* to be ill. She *was* ill.

Just because physical symptoms are brought on by emotional factors doesn't make them less real. When you tell your mother you are going away for a weekend, something within her tells her that you will never return, even though on an intellectual level she knows quite well that when the

◆

Let's face it: When your parent gets sick as a way of holding you close, she is not pretending. She really is sick.

weekend is over you will reappear just as you always have. This throws her into a panic and causes her symptoms. The pains of stomach distress hurt just as much when they are caused by emotions as by something she eats.

Once you understand something about what makes your parent tick, there are specific actions you can take when you're planning vacations. If you are going away for a short time, such as a long weekend, just don't tell her

◆

You can find ways to take vacations and ease your parent's anxiety at the same time.

that you are going away. Call from wherever you are and pretend that you are home, tired out, or not feeling well. Nobody likes to tell someone a fib, even a little one, especially to their mother. But this tactic will protect your mother from being attacked by her own feelings, if only temporarily, and will allow you to get the respite you need.

Of course, this strategy is not practical if you are going away for an extended period of time or are going to be at such a distance that you can't return quickly if necessary. In this case, you're going to have to tell the unvarnished truth. Here is how Morton did it under our guidance.

MORTON: Mother, tomorrow morning Greta and I are going to Phoenix, Arizona for two weeks. We . . .

ROSE: [*interrupts her son, takes a big sigh, and puts her head down*] I don't know what I am going to do.

MORTON: I know it will be hard for you. You have counted on my visits every week, and I won't be here in person for you for the next two weeks. I've thought about how we can still stay connected. We will call you from Phoenix and we will also send you postcards.

ROSE: [*takes another sigh and puts her hand over her heart*] Morton, darling. I'm not feeling so good. I'm getting sick.

MORTON: I'm sorry you're not feeling well. [*He stops and waits. At this point he is trying to give her some empathy. Any additional message would minimize her feelings.*]

ROSE: [*Says nothing. Continues to have her head down and have no eye contact with her son.*]

At this point Morton lets a few minutes pass. He goes in the kitchen, collects himself, and makes his mother and himself some coffee. He puts it on the table next to her before speaking.

MORTON: Mom, here's some coffee. [*Rose picks up her head.*] Sharon and the baby are going to visit you tomorrow. And during the week, my friend Sandra's mother, Betty, will come by. She would love to join you for lunch. In fact, she's looking for a retirement residence herself and is thinking of moving here.

ROSE: She's not going to like it here. The people are cold.

MORTON: Well, you can fill her in. She wants to hear everything about the place.

ROSE: I don't feel well.

MORTON: I feel so bad for you. [*He goes and gets her calender and fills in where he will be and when, and the dates of the visits he has arranged and shows it to his mother.*]

ROSE: [*She puts it on her lap and looks up at her son with a very sad face.*]

MORTON: [*He takes her hand.*] Mom, I'll call you when we land so you'll know we arrived okay.

The first thing to note about this conversation is that it took place just before Morton left on his trip. This gave Rose a minimum amount of time to get all nerved up. Then he told her his itinerary and when he was going where. He told her he would keep in touch and he arranged for substitute visitors during his absence. He didn't tell her this, but he also arranged for some extra attention from the people at the retirement residence.

Note how sometimes saying less is better. In the past whenever she said she was sick, Morton would launch into a tirade against his mother. This time he kept his cool and listened quietly in a kind and sympathetic way. He knows he can't make her complaints go away. But he can offer her his comfort.

The situation facing Morton and his mother was, of course, broader than this vacation problem. Rose seemed to be having trouble adjusting to her new environment, and this, too, was a source of great stress to her and her children. She was also feeling grief over the loss of her old home and environment. This is not easy for anyone, especially a person such as Rose, who will, at times, regret the move deeply and place the blame on her son and daughter-in-law. We will see later that people with this type of personality invariably blame others for everything that goes wrong in their lives.

Lifelong Dependency

Bea and Rose are very dependent people and have been this way all their lives. While they both demonstrated many of the difficult behaviors in the questionnaire at the beginning of the book, the behavior pattern that stood out most prominently in each was a lifelong clinging dependency.

How much dependency is too much? There are no absolutes, of course. Most of us are dependent on other people in one way or another. Everyone in a family unit takes care of some of the aspects of life and depends upon others to fulfill their needs in other areas. In particular, many women in the preliberation generations depended upon their husbands in ways that cause today's women to look askance. Similarly, men, especially in the older age groups, may be completely dependent on their wives for the daily tasks of housekeeping.

But Bea is not dependent in this ordinary sense. She has tied herself tightly to her son and is panicked at the least suggestion that he might be loosening the knot. Al's failure to call at the expected time triggered fears in Bea that came out in the form of hostility. Rose's inability to tolerate Morton's brief vacations make her dependency even more obvious.

An important step in helping grownchildren come to terms with parents such as Bea and Rose is the recognition that these dependent behaviors are not new. Sure, the behaviors have become more extreme as the years have gone by, but an objective look at the past shows that the patterns have been there all along since childhood.

The simple recognition that your parent has been difficult all her life helps you understand that your parent's difficult personality is driving the way she behaves and there is little she can do to control her behavior. This recognition can help a grownchild such as Al or Morton—or you, if your mother behaves in similar ways—end the fruitless task of trying to reason with their mothers, and it will help them become more sympathetic to their mothers' inner torments. One client coming to this recognition for the first time said, "I feel redeemed knowing that my mother is behaving this way because of her personality and not because of anything I did." With this new understanding she was able to extend herself more to her mother.

What makes a person behave in these dependent ways? One commonly held explanation is that some people have an underlying feeling of abandonment going back to events of early childhood—events that were real or events perceived as real. A mother who was hospitalized for an extended period of time or one who was depressed and withdrawn and couldn't pay enough attention to her baby are possible sources of abandonment feelings. It is easy to understand that if a person has such an uncontrollable fear of abandonment, he will do everything possible to cling to those near him as a way of guaranteeing they will not leave him.

Morton did not know enough of his mother's early history to be able to draw any conclusions about the source of her difficulties. Although he found the abandonment hypothesis plausible enough, he couldn't quite accept that his mother should feel he was abandoning her. She should know, he thought, that he was a faithful and devoted son who was always there for her. "But that is rational thinking," we told him. "When you tell her that you will return in a week, her head believes you, but her emotions convince her that you are leaving forever."

It was different with Al. He recalled his mother's story of how she'd had a baby brother who'd died when she was three years old. He had heard stories from others in the family about how Bea's mother had been preoccupied with the baby's illness for months and, after his death, had gone into a lengthy period of depression. Bea has no direct memory of these events, but she might well have an emotional memory of feeling abandoned by her mother, who was constantly tending to the sick brother and then preoccupied with grief. In our story, Bea's not hearing from her son at the appointed hour triggered anger and hostility, her automatic way of shielding herself from facing the depressing early memories. Understanding why she was behaving that way and the terror that she must be experiencing made Al and his wife feel less tyrannized. As they gained understanding of the kind of present circumstances that trigger her childhood abandonment reaction, their feelings of anger toward her abated enough for them to deal with her more kindly.

Al, like Morton, found it hard to believe that his mother felt abandoned. He was a very good son, devoted to his mother by any rational standard. He showed her affection. He visited and called with regularity. He often took her out to dinner. He handled all her financial affairs. How could she consider this abandonment? Finally he was able to understand that his mother was not judging him rationally and that her attitudes were lifelong and had nothing at all to do with him personally. But once he did understand, he found it helpful both for his own peace of mind and for the positive effect of his changed attitude on his mother.

Eventually both Al and Morton came to feel better themselves once they appreciated viscerally that their mothers were not out to torment them, that as bad as they felt, their mothers felt worse. Rose and Bea are typical people with clinging personalities who somehow got by into middle age with defenses that were reasonably successful in helping them cope under most circumstances. They both married and brought up families. Sure, their behaviors may have put off other people, but their adoring husbands were there to compensate for that. Now in old age and widowed, with the added physical and emotional problems that everyone feels in the aging process, they feel even more burdened. They are their own worst enemies, and often freely admit it.

◆

Expect a parent with lifelong dependency to suffer over separations

There is never a single strategy for dealing with dependent behaviors. Nor are hostility and physical illness the only ways in which this excessive dependence shows up. Others try for attention by continually requesting others to do things for them that they are fully able to do by themselves. Since no two people are alike in all respects, the steps taken have to be adapted to each individual. But whatever the approach, you should always appreciate that people with this personality suffer from being unable to control their extreme reactions when they anticipate a separation, even a brief one, from those upon whom they depend.

Dependency Can Show up for the First Time in Later Years

The same kinds of dependent behaviors that we have seen in Bea and Rose sometimes show up for the first time later in life. The combined effects of certain later-life traumas together with the normal assaults of the aging process can throw a person into a position of dependency. However, even though this group of people may behave as Bea and Rose do, they may be fundamentally different. This difference is crucial, because later-life dependency may be temporary and, if so, needs to be handled differently. Grownchildren are often stymied by this newly dependent behavior and don't know how to deal with it. It is hard to come to terms with a new trait, different from the one the grownchild had been accustomed to all his or her life. But, as with lifelong dependency, understanding the source of the behavior goes a long way in helping to guide your reactions both for your sake and your parent's.

How can you tell when the new dependency behaviors may moderate or even go away? If the cause is a chronic, progressive illness such as Alzheimer's disease, Parkinson's disease, or severe diabetes, then the associated personality changes are likely to remain and the grownchild is best advised to

◆

Later-life dependency caused by certain traumas can benefit from a different approach.

be guided by the tips earlier in the chapter for lifelong dependency. However when the cause is a medical condition such as the after effects of a mild to moderate stroke or heart surgery or the emotional reactions to the death of a spouse or other close relative or friend, or another kind of loss—for example, a move from one city to another, or even from one residence to another—then there is hope the dependency will decrease.

Here are three illustrations of potentially reversible later-life dependency:

ESTHER MOVED
◆

Esther developed a small business in Boston after her husband died forty-five years earlier. Now at age seventy-nine the business started to fail and her knees gave out at about the same time. She was convinced by her family to move

*into a retirement home in Virginia near her eldest daughter.
She missed her business terribly. Being naturally shy, she had
difficulty making friends both in her retirement home and
elsewhere. Although she had never made close friends during
all her years in Boston, she had loved the contacts with her
customers. She missed that aspect of her life.*

*Esther now complains of boredom and loneliness, inter-
rupts her daughter's business meetings with calls throughout
the day, and wants to squeeze herself into her daughter's
personal life as well. She criticizes other residents in her retirement home and blames her daughter for moving her. Her
daughter feels guilty and helpless about how to deal with
her mother.*

◆

SYLVIA HAD HEART BYPASS SURGERY
◆

*Sylvia was recovering nicely from heart bypass surgery. Her
doctor had assured her and her children that she was able
to resume the same lifestyle as before her illness. The problem
was that she was unwilling to do things for herself such as
showering, dressing, and preparing meals, all of which she
had done easily before. Instead, she turned to her daughter
for almost everything and demanded almost continuous attention. It was beginning to wear on her daughter. She was
puzzled by her mother's new dependency and worn out trying to balance her own family responsibilities with caring
for her mother. She began to lose patience and realized that
something had to be done. Here is how she handled it.*

◆

DAUGHTER: Mom, I'm wearing myself out between work and
giving you the extra help you need. Why don't we get a
helper to assist you around the house until you feel like
your old self again?

SYLVIA: Honey, I didn't realize you were getting so tired. I guess
I have been relying on you a lot. I'm not used to relying

on anyone, but since my surgery, my whole world has changed.

DAUGHTER: I know, Mom. The doctor says you'll be needing help for a few more weeks. I wonder if that wonderful lady who helped your friend Susan after her gall bladder surgery is available?

It turned out that this "wonderful lady" was a trained nurse's aide who was able to work with Sylvia to become more independent in her daily living skills, like bathing, dressing, and even preparing meals for herself.

Because Sylvia's dependency occurred late in life, it was potentially reversible, in contrast to the lifelong dependency shown by Rose and Bea. She could really listen to her daughter's explanation of how worn out she was. She recognized that her needs were greater now than they were before her illness and could understand how demanding this could be on her daughter's busy schedule. Rationality worked.

Bringing in the trained nurse's aide accomplished its purpose of relieving the strain on Sylvia's daughter. But there was another benefit as well. The heart surgery left Sylvia very fearful. In her fear she found comfort in leaning on her daughter. Even when she was physically able to resume her former lifestyle, she was afraid to do so. But with her daughter's encouragement and the security of having a dependable aide at her side, Sylvia was able to regain her independent spirit.

FRANK'S WIFE DIED
◆

Frank's wife recently died of cancer. The two of them had had a very loving marriage and an active life together for forty-eight years. They were best friends. Their three grown-children would describe their parents as two very independent people who each could stand on their own two feet. Now Dad is limping along.

It is seven months since Frank's loss, and he still sits morosely at home. He refuses invitations to go out with his

*friends and wants only his daughters and son to visit. His
children find it even more disturbing that he can't make the
simplest decisions of daily living. He looks to his children to
decide which day of the week the house cleaner should come
or to which charity he should donate money. Then when
they try to help him with his decision making, he finds fault
with their advice. This makes them feel angry and rejected
at the same time. Their impulse is to withdraw from him,
but they can't do that because he obviously needs them more
than ever.*

◆

Grieving Later-Life Losses

◆

Newly dependent
behaviors can be
expected to wear off.

The most important thread that ties
these three situations together is the
fact that Esther, Sylvia, and Frank each
underwent traumatic events that
changed their lives and are undergoing
an adjustment period that had a beginning and, most likely,
will have an end. The emotional recovery time from a move,
illness, or death of spouse can easily take a year at the least.
But even if it takes longer than you think it should, don't give
up hope. The newly dependent behavior can be expected to
wear off.

In the three examples, it is fair to characterize the events
that preceded the newfound dependencies as major. Sometimes the events may appear to be less consequential, such as
a fall, a bout with the flu, or the death of a favorite dog. Yet
these situations of loss and change can also be the final straw
that pulls one downward, and results in a state of greater dependency than before.

When a person goes through such experiences, you can
expect a grieving process to take place. Grieving is not just
for mourners such as Frank. Esther and Sylvia are also grieving
because they, too, are dealing with major losses: Esther has

lost her home, acquaintances, and her role as business owner; Sylvia has lost her vital, active, and healthy self.

In an older person, these losses tend to be multiple. For example, Esther not only lost her business but much of her mobility due to arthritis, a loss of a different kind. The move to be near her daughter meant giving up—and losing—her more independent lifestyle.

It is understandable, then, that Esther, Sylvia, and Frank would suffer changes. All three are coping with their losses by depending on their children for comfort and support and to fill the voids. Chances are they will grieve their losses normally and that time will help. How different this is from people with lifelong dependencies, such as Bea and Rose, who find it hard to grieve because doing so brings back the early abandonment issues. (See Chapter 8 for a more complete discussion of loss and grief.) The tips for dealing with parents with later-life dependency will flow from understanding that these individuals are experiencing a temporary setback and until they regain their equilibrium, they will feel and act more dependent than they and their families are accustomed to.

Dealing with Later-Life Dependency

Now that you know that your parent, after a move or other loss, needs to go through a grieving period that lasts a year or more, you can be more patient and supportive rather than alarmed or angry. Here are some other ideas.

Unlike dealing with a parent with lifelong dependency, you can use reason with your parent. For example, Sylvia's daughter said to her mother, "Mom, I'm wearing myself out be-

◆

Have a discussion with your parent. Reasoning works.

tween work and giving you the extra help you need. Why don't we get a helper to assist you around the house until you feel like your old self again?"

◆

Find substitute roles that bring satisfaction.

Esther's daughter might brainstorm with her to see if there is a substitute role for her, such as being a receptionist or welcomer at the retirement home. Perhaps she could become a volunteer giving telephone reassurance to homebound seniors. In these roles she would be offering a service similar to those in her former life as a businesswoman. If Esther could be persuaded to take on one of these roles, it might help her to minimize her dependency.

◆

Sympathy and a hug won't hurt.

If Frank's daughters were to nag him into socializing with his old friends, he might withdraw even more and feel angry for their lack of sensitivity to his grief. The most comforting words to Frank during his grief period might be, "Dad, we know how terribly you miss Mom." And a hug wouldn't hurt.

◆

Don't tell your parent what to do.

You know how you don't like to be told by your parent what to do with your life? Well, the same holds for your parents not liking your direct advice. For Sylvia's daughter to push her mom to shower and bathe herself would not be well received. Convincing her mother to accept a nurse's aide was an effective way of introducing a neutral third party.

Finally, a word about you, the grownchild. All your life you had a vibrant and independent parent. Now she is anything but. You don't like to see your parent so dependent. Not only is it hard for you to see her suffering physically and emotionally, but caring for her may be just as physically and emotionally burdensome for you as it is for the children of parents with lifelong dependency. And so the advice we gave earlier in the chapter is just as applicable to you. Take care of yourself. Do what you think is reasonable and try to keep from taking on more than you can comfortably handle. Though the advice is the same, the approach can be very different: You can explain your decision to your recently dependent parent and discuss it with her, something that is less likely to work when your parent has been dependent all her life.

2

THE WORLD IN BLACK AND WHITE

TURNOFF BEHAVIORS

When your parent:

◆ tends to view others as all good or all bad. Sometimes the same person can be all good one day and all bad the next.
◆ is extremely negative and complains of unhappiness.
◆ is hypercritical of others and hypersensitive to criticism or blame.
◆ is tactless.
◆ has to be "right" all the time.
◆ is angry and hostile, while blaming others for the same characteristics.
◆ has temper tantrums, e.g., throws things, or uses abusive language.
◆ is distrustful and suspicious, sometimes to the point of paranoia.
◆ pushes people away, or even cuts off the relationship.

The grownchildren of the last chapter sought out professional help because of the way their parents acted out their feelings of dependency—hostility in the first example, and illness in the next. In the examples the family members were distraught because of behaviors in their mothers they could not understand. Until they received some help, they didn't know what to do with their own frustration and anger. Then, with our guidance and insight into their parents' behaviors, they were able to deal with their mothers in more constructive ways.

Those examples of dependency are, of course, only a few
of the behaviors that bring family members to us and other
geriatric counselors on a daily basis. The behaviors in the second category of the questionnaire at the beginning of the book
can be even more distressful to grownchildren. When you consider the examples in this and the next chapter, you will understand why we use the word "turnoff" to characterize the
impact on others. The first of these "turnoffs"—viewing those
around them in black and white—is such a common difficult
behavior that we devote this chapter to it.

A "GOOD" SON BECOMES "BAD"

◆

◆

A mother alienates all
her children by her
"black-and-white" view
of the world.

*Patty finally screwed up enough cour-
age to dial her mother, Mary. These
telephone calls were painful and always had been. "How are you,
Mother?" she said. The response was
cold and perfunctory. Patty continued
on an upbeat tone: "I saw Steve and Hope yesterday. Steve
just got a promotion—more money and prestige. He's a go-
getter, that brother of mine."*

*"He knows how to go and get for himself, all right," was
the reply. "What did I ever do to deserve such treatment,
after all I did for him," she continued. "You're always on his
side. I suppose you think it was my fault that he moved out."*

*Patty snapped right back: "Why are you so angry,
Mother?" Patty was taken aback by this outburst, even
though experience should have taught her to expect it.
"You're the one who's angry, not me," was Mary's response.*

*Try as she might, there was little that Patty could do to
elevate the tone of the conversation. She decided there was
little point continuing, and she ended it with, "I love you,
Mother." Mary did not respond.*

*Patty's closing words came hard. Her mother was indeed
difficult to love. Now in her sixties, she was in good health
and lived alone. All four of her children lived within a few*

miles of her home, yet Patty was the only one who called or visited with any regularity. The others found the relationship so difficult that the easiest thing for them was to keep away as much as possible.

Steve was the last to break away. He and Hope had married a few years before. He had a degree in business administration, but had been unable to find work for a long time. Finally he found a job with a major corporation, but at a very low salary. Mother suggested that her son and daughter-in-law come to live in her house. Steve viewed the offer as a mixed blessing. Sure, he would welcome the free rent. But he feared he would have to pay a heavy emotional price for it. And, as it turned out, his fears were justified.

For Steve, going to college was a liberating experience. As long as he lived at home, his mother would make constant demands upon him, treating him, in effect, as an indentured servant. She never expressed any gratitude when he took care of household chores and drove her around on errands. She expected it. As she kept saying, it was the least he could do to repay her for everything she did for him. At the same time, she would tell outsiders what a wonderful son she had. "Those daughters of mine are only for themselves, but my son, Steve, is different."

Thus, the notion of moving back with her, this time with a wife, filled him with some trepidation. He finally agreed, thinking she would be nicer to him now that he was married.

But nothing changed. Once he was back in the house she began to have the same expectations as before. And she was jealous of all the time he spent with Hope, muttering under her breath about "that selfish girl." Finally, he had his fill. Free rent or not, he and Hope were leaving. "How could you do this to me?" was all she could say when he finally told her his plans. As the weeks went by, she didn't say another word. She bristled with a new fierce determination, giving both Steve and Hope the cold shoulder. Finally when the moving day arrived, she claimed she was never told about it. As they left the house she yelled with fierce anger, "You'll see! You'll never get along without me."

Now it was three years later and Mary still had not gotten over her resentment when Steve left her. The son on whom she had placed so much hope had turned out no better, from her point of view, than her three daughters: They had all abandoned their mother in her later years.

A GRANDMOTHER REJECTS HER FAVORITE GRANDSON

Here is another example of similar behavior.

◆

Betty was an embittered woman. She barely tolerated her son and two daughters. But then there was Jeff, her grandson. Jeff was "special," as she told everyone who would listen. His mother was ungrateful to her, uncaring and unloving. But Jeff understood her and wanted to spend time with her.

Jeff and his family lived just a few blocks from Grandma. He was always at her house. All during his high school years, he would run errands for her, and sit there with her for hours talking over the events of his day and listening to her complaints.

Near the end of his senior year, Jeff was admitted with a full scholarship to a college about two hundred miles away. All that spring he had waited patiently for word from the several colleges to which he had applied. On each visit to Grandma's, he would talk about his hopes and aspirations. As soon as he heard the good news, he ran over to Grandma to share it with her. Her reaction took him by surprise. "Why didn't you apply to a college near home?" she demanded in a hostile tone. "You know I did," he said, "but they didn't give me a scholarship. Besides, this college has a much better business school."

Betty was now bristling with hostility. "You didn't think of your grandma when you made that decision, did you!" Jeff was taken aback. His grandmother had never talked to him in such a tone of voice before. It was the way she talked

*to his mother, but never to Jeff. He left in a puzzled mood.
The next day he returned only to find that she refused to let
him in the house.*

*Jeff went to that out-of-state college. He called his grand-
mother shortly after his arrival, but she hung up on him.
When he returned home on his first vacation, he tried again
but she still refused to talk to him. It remained that way
all through his college years. The wonderful grandchild had
become bad. And he didn't have the faintest idea what had
caused his grandmother to turn against him so abruptly.*

◆

Why Some People Turn Hot and Cold

Mary and Betty are typical of many older people whose grownchildren come to us for help. "What can I do when my mother
acts this way? Nothing I do or say ever helps," is the common complaint.

Mary and Betty lack the perspective that most of us have
of viewing their children and others as human beings with
weaknesses as well as strengths. Most of us continue to accept
our parents, our children and, especially, our grandchildren,
even when they behave in ways we don't like. But some people find it difficult to see things in any but black-and-white
terms. For them there is no gray scale. People are either all
one way or all the other way. Thus to Mary, her daughters
were bad and her son was good, until he did something that
made him bad. This extreme reaction was even more obvious
with Jeff. He was the good grandson despite his bad mother.
We can understand a grandmother's disappointment when a
beloved grandchild leaves town for college. Most would have
balanced this disappointment with pride in the young boy's
development. Betty couldn't strike this balance. The coin had
flipped. Jeff had become another deserter.

The technical name for this "black-and-white" behavior is
splitting, and it almost always accompanies the range of other
behavior patterns in the questionnaire.

◆

Seeing the world in black and white is called "splitting."

Splitting, like extreme dependency, comes from a feeling of abandonment

We saw in Chapter 1 that lifelong dependency is often caused by feelings of abandonment that stem from the earliest years. Sometimes the source of this abandonment is to be found in events that inhibit the normal process of separation of a baby from the mother. No one knows for sure exactly how and why this happens in any given instance.

Under any circumstances, a child has ambivalent feelings toward his mother in this separation process. On the one hand, he is striving for independence—you can see it in the eyes of the one-year-old widening his very own physical world by taking his first steps away and then back to his mother, and in the child in "the terrible twos" constantly seeking to do things himself free of parental control. Most parents can cite examples, such as one mother who told how Billy, her two-year-old, mindful of the rule that he had to hold hands crossing the street, rejected his mother's hand and held his own. At the same time, however, the toddler is careful not to stray too far away, always watching to be sure that his mother is there. In a baby's primitive view, his mother is split into two people: a "bad," depriving mother from whom he is seeking more independence and a "good," nurturing mother who is always there if he should need support and comfort as he widens his horizons.

The normal child continues this process of separation from his mother throughout childhood and adolescence, and gradually the good mother and bad mother images fuse together so that he eventually accepts her as an integrated human being with strengths and weaknesses. But when something happens in those first three years to interfere with this normal separation process, the child's emotional development may become affected.

While other children gradually are becoming more independent, this child remains with the emotional makeup of the toddler as he continues to seek comfort from his "good" mother to overcome the depression resulting from being abandoned by his "bad" mother. Thus, instead of developing a mature understanding of his mother as a multifaceted human being as he grows older, he becomes stuck with the infantile response to separateness with its inability to resolve the split between the "good" and "bad" mothers.

Later in life, this person may transfer this love/hate relationship from his mother to a spouse, and, still later, to his own child. But the split view of the world usually remains, touching on all relationships.

Mary and Betty both behave in ways that suggest they suffer from these feelings of abandonment. That is why Mary cannot interact with her children as many mothers do. Steve's "walking out" on her triggers an emotional recollection of the bad, depriving mother. Betty experienced similar abandonment feelings when her grandson left town to go to college.

Expect a person who has always seen the world in black and white to continue to do so when something happens that triggers feelings of abandonment. Often the trigger is separation or impending separation, i.e., anything that distances or threatens to distance the individual from those she depends on. Here are some examples of common triggers.

- A son calls off a dinner date because of a late business meeting.
- A grandchild forgets to send a card or call on Mother's Day.
- A daughter strains her back and has to postpone a visit by a day.
- A home helper takes the weekend off, and the agency sends in a replacement.
- A son goes off on a weeklong business trip.

Whatever the trigger, the mother's instinctive thought process follows this kind of sequence.

- My son is the only good person I can depend upon.
- He is going away for a week.
- Now he is deserting me.

- He is deserting me because I must have done something bad.
- I'm down in the dumps, and I can't bear those feelings.
- I am not bad, he is.
- I'll show him what it's like to feel like this.

If your parent responds to you and others in these ways, you should recognize she is not attacking you deliberately. Rather she is defending herself from a perceived emotional threat. It is self-protection.

◆

Splitting is a matter of self-protection.

The splitter feels worse than you do.

Always remember that as bad and helpless as you may feel when you are the object of your parent's splitting, deep down your parent feels worse than you do. As you can see from the above thought processes, people such as Mary and Betty convert "good" people into "bad" as a way of getting rid of their own painful feelings. This is called *projection*. We have more to say about this a little later in the chapter.

◆

Don't be surprised if your parent flips and flops.

"I never know what to expect from my mother," is a common complaint we hear from some grownchildren when they come for help. "Yesterday, I was the best son in the world. I could do no wrong, and today I am 'heartless,' " he lamented. "I can't even figure out what I did to deserve such treatment." Then there was the woman whose mother-in-law greeted her one day with hostile coldness as soon as she stepped into her retirement residence apartment. It was a big surprise (even though it had happened before) because the director of the retirement facility had met her on the way in and told her how only the day before her mother-in-law had engaged in a daughter-in-law bragging contest with another resident.

These examples show that people with a tendency to split can do so often and repeatedly. They may turn against a grownchild or other person overnight and then switch back to acceptance with no apparent provocation, a mood shift that reflects the emotional instability of someone with a difficult personality. This unpredictability is particularly hard on the family members. If you have had the experience of being a parent, you can readily see how this on-again/off-again behavior resembles that of the two-year-old loving her mother one minute and hating her the next, just as if the mother were two separate individuals.

What to Do When Your Parent Turns Hot and Cold

The key to a satisfactory relationship with a parent who acts in such seemingly irrational ways is to recognize that her behavior is beyond her control.

♦
The splitter cannot help it.

People such as Mary and Betty split because they do not know how to moderate their behavior. They are pulled to react in extremes, *this* way or *that* way. They don't understand "a little bit of this and a little bit of that." If this description fits your parent, you can expect her to go into her split mode automatically when threatened by separation, and you can expect to become the "bad guy" no matter what you say or do.

The incident between Betty and her grandson is a case in point. The teenager was flabbergasted when his grandmother got angry with him instead of rejoicing with him when she heard that he had won a scholarship to a fine university. Another lonely grandmother might have told her grandson of her mixed feelings. "Jeff, darling, it will be very lonely for me without you around all the time. But I'm so proud of you for winning the scholarship. I know that you will do well." Betty's "all-or-nothing" personality didn't let her react in that way.

Recognize that people with all-or-nothing personalities have trouble interacting with more than one person at a time. They feel safer in one-to-one relationships. Interacting with two peo-

♦
Keep your relationship one-on-one as much as possible.

ple at once will inevitably lead to splitting her positive and
negative feelings between the two. Keep your relationship one-
on-one as much as possible, avoiding a three-person triad. For
Steve to bring home a wife is a setup for a good/bad split.

Remember how Jeff tried to tell his
grandmother all the reasons that led up
to his selection of a college? It didn't
work. You can't argue rationally with
people who feel the way Betty feels.
They commonly defend themselves in
some of the following ways that defy rational discussion:

◆

You can't argue
rationally with a
splitter.

Denial. "I never said such a thing," or [*enraged*]: "I am
not angry!" For example, Mary denied that she knew Steve
was leaving and blamed him for not telling her.

Projection—ascribing one's own feelings to others.
"You're the one who is angry. Don't accuse me of anger!"
This is exactly what happened during the telephone conversa-
tion that Patty had with her mother.

**Selective Hearing—blocking out what is unwelcome
and hearing what she wants to hear.** For example, Betty's
grandson, Jeff, had discussed all the colleges with her, but she
closed her ears and didn't hear him.

This splitting behavior is very hard to take, and it is understandable that some grownchildren just can't tolerate it. Some
grownchildren react to a parent who behaves in these ways
by pulling away. Others placate her by doing everything the
parent wants. If you have reacted in either of these extreme
ways, you should recognize that you are mimicking your parent's behavior. In other words, *you* are splitting. It's no wonder—you have a great role model!

You don't have to fall into this trap. There is a better
approach both for your parent and for you, but navigating this
path is not easy. We illustrated some of the dos and don'ts of
this approach using the phone conversation between Patty and
her mother. We helped Patty role-play with two variations on
this conversation in which we played Patty, and Patty played
her mother.

First, we repeat the actual conversation. Recall that at the moment of their phone conversation, Patty's mother was treating her son Steve as the "bad guy" and her daughter Patty as the "good guy."

ORIGINAL TELEPHONE CONVERSATION

PATTY: I saw Steve and Hope yesterday. Steve just got a promotion—more money and prestige. He's a go-getter, that brother of mine.

MOTHER: What did I ever do to deserve such treatment, after all I did for him. You're always on his side. I suppose you think it was my fault that he moved out.

PATTY: Why are you so angry, Mother?

MOTHER: You're the one who's angry, not me.

Patty knew from experience that her comment about her mother getting angry was a mistake because her mother would feel criticized. Nevertheless, Patty could have done worse. In the following role play, Patty tries to reason with her mother and, of course, fails miserably.

UNSUCCESSFUL THERAPY ROLE PLAY—USING REASON (THERAPIST AS PATTY, PATTY AS HER MOTHER)

PATTY: I saw Steve yesterday. He just got a promotion—more money and prestige. He's a go-getter, that brother of mine.

MOTHER: What did I ever do to deserve such treatment, after all I did for him. You're always on his side. I suppose you think it was my fault that he moved out.

PATTY: *[trying to be logical]* Steve and Hope needed to be on their own.

MOTHER: *[interpreting her daughter's remark as taking Steve's side against her]* He's an ungrateful son. This is what I get after all I did for him. Why do you always take his part?

PATTY: *[continuing to be logical and inflaming her mother still more]* I wonder why you are so angry at Steve? Maybe you're really still angry at your brother and are taking it out on your son.

MOTHER: *[now in a rage]* Patty, your brother is no good. He

is just like the rest of them. Now I can see that you're no
better than the others.

PATTY: *[still continuing to be logical]* Oh, Mother, settle down
now. I'm sure you'll feel better about Steve after you think
about this overnight.

◆

Don't try to reason
with a "splitting"
parent. It only makes
things worse.

Don't defend the "bad
guy." You will become
a bad guy yourself.

Don't try to play
psychiatrist.

In this worst-case scenario, Patty
had the best of intentions but did everything wrong. Using reason and logic
not only made her mother angrier than
she was before, but also succeeded in
putting Patty in her mother's doghouse
by defending Patty's brother. A person
like Patty's mother, especially when
under stress, can't listen to reason.
Patty made things even worse by trying
to give her mother her theory as to
why her mother behaved as she did,

and her mother took it as a personal attack. A better approach
is not to try to convince her of anything, but simply to let her
know that you are there for her, in other words, to validate
her. This is the approach of the second role play between
Patty and her counselor.

SUCCESSFUL THERAPY ROLE PLAY—USING VALIDATION
(THERAPIST AS PATTY, PATTY AS HER MOTHER)

PATTY: I saw Steve yesterday. He just got a promotion—more
money and prestige. He's a go-getter, that brother of mine.

MOTHER: What did I ever do to deserve such treatment, after
all I did for him. You're always on his side. I suppose you
think it was my fault that he moved out.

PATTY: *[validating her mother's feelings]* No, I only know it
was hard on you when he did.

MOTHER: You don't know the half of it. Steve has been awful
to me.

PATTY: *[refusing to take sides]* This has been terrible for you,
Mom.

MOTHER: What did I do to deserve this?

PATTY: *[treating her mother sympathetically]* I'm sorry that this is happening. You don't need this upset.

This time Patty did everything right. She knew nothing good would ever come out of criticizing her mother's behavior. And so she validated her mother by responding sympathetically to her without agreeing or disagreeing with the substance of her remarks. She was careful to avoid inserting herself into the mother-son relationship. Above all, she let her mother know that whatever the circumstances, she would always be there for her.

◆

Don't argue; validate.

Let your parent know that you are there for her.

This last hypothetical role-play scenario was successful because it came from an understanding of her mother's lifelong reaction to separation issues. Patty was able to use this validation approach when she called her mother a few days later and was delighted with the results. As she later told her therapist, "It didn't get worse like it usually does. In fact, we were able to have lunch together that day and completely change the topic. I didn't feel so awful about myself, either. Usually I berate myself for yelling at my mother. Now I feel for her a little more. She really gets into a terrible snit with herself."

Patty felt a lot better as a result of her counseling sessions. If you have a parent like Patty's, you, too, will need all the insights, support, and tips you can get, and you will benefit, as Patty did, from a counselor or in a support group. But keep in mind that sometimes nothing works. Don't blame anyone. Your parent is driven to behave this way because of something going on inside her beyond her control. It's not your fault, and it's not hers. A counselor can help you come to terms with this reality.

◆

Avert a crisis. Get counseling or go to a support group.

While there are some grownchildren like Patty who come to us for help in getting along better with their difficult parents, there are many others in similar situations who don't think of getting professional help until there is a specific problem relating to the parent's care, and it is only then that the grownchild has the opportunity to obtain help on the behavioral as well as the practical problems. For example, you may be in a situation similar to Patty's with a relatively young mother in good health but with a difficult personality. You may have kept away from her as much as possible. As the years go by, chances are that her health will suffer and she will be less able to manage independently. When this occurs, she will need to look to her children for some help, and you may be stepping back into the picture more out of a sense of responsibility than of love. You may want your mother to move closer to you, perhaps to a retirement residence. Like most people, you may not be aware of the full spectrum of housing options for older people, and may seek out a geriatric health professional for help in this area. Under any circumstances, making a move to another city or even a change in housing in the same location can be a source of great stress to the older person. But when your mother has been difficult all her life and you have estranged yourself, it is easy to see how such a difficult situation can turn into a family crisis. That's why it is so important to get help before the situation reaches a crisis stage.

TURNING AGAINST A PERFECT HELPER

A person with a tendency to split does not confine her black-and-white behaviors to her children and other relatives. It is often a helper who has to bear the brunt of these reactions, and when this happens it becomes particularly stressful to a grownchild. Here is a typical example.

◆

Nancy came to our offices at her wit's end. Her mother could not get by in her own apartment without the services of a helper. Well-trained helpers, sympathetic to older people, are not always easy to find, and this daughter has spent a great deal of time interviewing people until she finally made a choice. The woman turned out to be ideal in every respect.

The mother came to be so dependent upon her that she would sit there worrying about her each morning until she came through the door. Then, one day, the helper was late due to a traffic accident. The mother became so panicky that she pounced on her helper when she finally arrived, told her that she was no good at all if she couldn't come on time, and proceeded to fire her.

Nancy was back to where she started. Once again she would have to go through the difficult job of finding a satisfactory helper. Once again she went through the interviewing process until she found another person. Then, of course, the same thing happened. The daughter was on the verge of running out of qualified candidates for the job when she came in for our help. The situation now was worse than ever. "My mother wants me to be there each day," she lamented. "She really needs someone. I don't want to do this, but I'll worry about her being alone. What should I do?"

◆

Here are some of the words of advice we gave Nancy about her situation. If you are in a situation similar to Nancy's, they will apply to you as well.

Don't assume all the burden of hiring the helper. Give your parent some choice in the hiring process by having her interview the prospective helpers. This will remind her that the helper is *hers* and not *yours*. One client recognized that her mother, who had some dementia, was not up to the job of interviewing and then hiring all by herself. This grownchild solved the problem by interviewing several people herself, selecting the two leading candidates. She then had her mother interview the two people and make the final selection.

◆

Get your parent involved in the process of hiring helpers.

When you hire a helper, be sure to tell her how your mother behaves, how your mother blows hot and cold for no apparent reason, and that she should

◆

Explain your parent's behavior to the helper.

expect to be praised one minute and scolded the next. And, above all, explain that your mother behaves this way because she can't help it—it's nothing personal. Point out that your mother might get so angry at her that she might fire her, but that the next day she may very well want to rehire her, so the helper should be ready to call the next day to see if your mother wants her to return. Keep the lines of communication open. Talk to the helper frequently and be prepared to shore her up when your parent has an especially bad day and takes it out on her. Tell her she is free to call you for emotional support. But be sure that this is kept confidential so as not to make your parent suspicious that the two of you are allied against her. Then you will both be in her doghouse.

♦

Get your parent's doctor involved.

If your mother's doctor agrees, have him tell her very firmly that she cannot be left alone. She is more likely to listen to an authority figure such as a doctor than a grownchild. Nancy convinced her mother to see her doctor, and he explained to her how her medical problems made a helper essential. Then he formalized his comment by putting it down on a prescription pad.

George Smith, MD
1400 MAIN ST.
GREENVILLE, NEW JERSEY
(609) 555-4567

October 10,1998

Mrs. Elizabeth Price must have a helper 24 hours a day for medical reasons.

George Smith, MD

The note was simple and to the point. Nancy put it up on the bulletin board right near her mother's favorite seat. Every time she was about to fire the helper, Nancy took it off the board and handed it to her so that she could read it firsthand. Furthermore, the doctor told Nancy that he was willing to see her mother if this system was not working. His backup plan was to tell his patient that if she couldn't retain the helpers, he would prescribe an assisted-living facility.

♦

Don't let yourself get trapped into playing the helper role.

Remember, for this to work successfully you have to resolve and let your mother know that you will not take the place of or even fill in for a helper. So if your parent turns against her helper and sends her away, don't fill in or rush out too quickly to find a replacement. Give your mother a chance to realize how much she needs assistance.

3

NEGATIVE AND OTHER TURNOFF BEHAVIORS

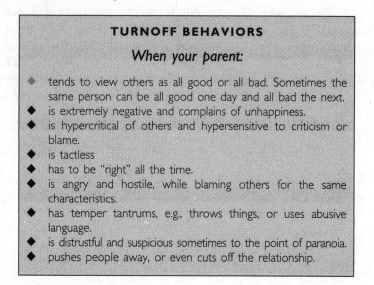

TURNOFF BEHAVIORS

When your parent:

◆ tends to view others as all good or all bad. Sometimes the same person can be all good one day and all bad the next.
◆ is extremely negative and complains of unhappiness.
◆ is hypercritical of others and hypersensitive to criticism or blame.
◆ is tactless
◆ has to be "right" all the time.
◆ is angry and hostile, while blaming others for the same characteristics.
◆ has temper tantrums, e.g., throws things, or uses abusive language.
◆ is distrustful and suspicious sometimes to the point of paranoia.
◆ pushes people away, or even cuts off the relationship.

If you know someone who behaves like the parents in the last chapter, chances are you stay away from him as much as you can—unless that person is your own parent who is getting older and needs you more and more as time goes on.

Seeing people as all good or all bad, the frustrating behavior called splitting, which we discussed in the previous chapter, is just one way of turning people off. There are other behaviors that can be just as aggravating. You only have to see the above list taken from the questionnaire to see why we call them *turnoffs,* that is, behaviors that make you want to stay away. People who act this way are basically very unhappy, and these behaviors are the way in which this unhappiness comes across to others.

Nothing demonstrates this more than their negative view of the world. When a young person is negative, we may be inclined to ignore it or even laugh it off. But when an older parent is negative, it can drive a grownchild up the wall, particularly when he knows the parent's negativity can be dangerous to her well-being. Some of the following vignettes show what we mean.

A MOTHER INSISTS ON STAYING PUT
◆

Elsie had been an unhappy person from her youngest days. She married and brought up a family, but her negative ways were trying to both her husband and children. Her husband, Harry, was very devoted, giving in to her to try to make her happy and placating her when things did not go her way. But no matter how hard he tried to make her happy, she managed to find something to complain about.

Then when her two children went off, one to college and the other to marry, Elsie slumped into even more unhappiness. It seemed as if Elsie were invested in being miserable. She criticized her husband for working so hard and not taking vacations, her children for not phoning on her birthday, and her neighbors for not giving her the name of their gardener.

Then, at age eighty-seven, Harry died, leaving Elsie a widow at age eighty-five. Her misery deepened during the illness preceding Harry's death, and she blamed Harry for working so hard and not taking care of himself. "If he had only taken vacations like other husbands, then this wouldn't have happened." And she blamed him for not showing her about their finances and all the details of household management, which made her unable to manage on her own.

Elsie had always leaned on Harry to plan and provide some level of social activity. Now with Harry gone and all the children out of town, she was lonely and miserable, espe-

cially in the winter when the bad weather kept her housebound. To top it off, her eyesight was beginning to fail, and she was no longer able to drive to the grocery store. She would call up her children and complain that she needed help but had nobody to help her. Her children lived so far away and weren't of any use to her. There were no other relatives nearby. Her neighbors were so "hateful"; they never offered to help her out.

Her children visited whenever they could to get a first-hand view of the situation. The children had recognized when their father died that it would be hard for their mother to remain in her home alone. They tried to talk to her about alternative arrangements, but she was unwilling to consider any change. Now that things were getting worse, they stepped up their efforts to get her to sell her house and move to a retirement community where she would not be so lonely and would be relieved of the household responsibilities. She refused to even consider the possibility. "Stop bugging me," she said, trembling with anger. "I don't need you or anyone else to tell me what to do." And under her breath she would say an often-repeated phrase: "You people are so hateful."

◆

Empathy Can Help

After six months of this steadily deteriorating situation, Elsie's daughter found herself spending more and more time away from her own family looking after her mother. Her frustration level finally got so high that she felt she had to seek help in coping with her mother and came to one of the workshops that we run for grownchildren and other caregivers.

Seeing that Elsie's negativity was an impenetrable barrier to rational discussion, we suggested another tack: Instead of arguing with your mother and losing all the arguments, try empathizing with her instead. This means letting her know that you understand how *she* feels about somebody or something without necessarily agreeing with her.

The advice worked. Here is an excerpt from a more recent conversation between Elsie and her daughter about the pros and cons of moving to a retirement home.

♦

Rather than arguing or defending yourself, try empathizing with your negative parent instead.

MOTHER: That place is too far from shopping.
DAUGHTER: I know you are used to such convenient shopping.
MOTHER: I know someone who lives there and I don't like her.
DAUGHTER: Uh-huh.
MOTHER: What am I going to do with all my things when I move into a small apartment?
DAUGHTER: I imagine it will be hard not taking everything with you, but if you want, I'll help you sort.

To the families' surprise, Elsie made the decision to move to the retirement home but kept saying she made a big mistake.

♦

For your sake and your parent's, don't try to force her to see your side.

MOTHER: I'm going to regret this decision for the rest of my life.
DAUGHTER: I'm sorry you feel this way.
MOTHER: I don't have a family like others have. You and your brother don't visit me together as a family.
DAUGHTER: I know it's a disappointment.

This style of communication may be new to you. You have probably tried to convince your parent of the brighter side of life. At other times you may have felt very angry at negative comments directed at you. However, if you work at trying to understand that this negative and critical behavior usually comes from your parent's own sense of inadequacy, you will stop trying to get her to see your side.

In fact, people such as Elsie have trouble allowing themselves to have pleasure, happiness, or contentment. At the same time, they often blame their displeasure on those closest to them. Rather than dealing with their bad feelings, they struggle to find some peace by getting rid of their feelings in a number of nonconstructive ways that leave them feeling even more miserable and alone. If you try to be empathic and support people like Elsie for their underlying misery, it will help them contain these negative feelings. You will not feel as if you are acting like your parent by also being negative and critical, and if you have children, you will have provided them with a positive role model.

The hardest thing for grownchildren with parents like Elsie is to hold their

◆

A statement such as "Let's not fuss over this" can help both of you.

tongues when confronted with such negativity. When you read this dialogue, you may have been tempted to say, "You should be lucky you have any family to visit." But that only would have antagonized her and filled the air with tension. Rather, the daughter's empathic response helped to allay her mother's negative outlook.

If you find yourself too angry to utter empathetic words, then try saying something like, "Let's not fuss over this." It's amazing how a simple act like this can defuse a tense situation and let you start afresh.

As we just saw, anger is often a natural reaction of a grownchild to a negative parent. And if the grownchild gets angry, so will the parent, and the verbal fisticuffs that follow will do no one any good. These fights are not inevitable. When we tell this to our clients, they seem incredulous. This nonbelligerent path comes from putting empathy into action. Here is something that one grownchild has learned to tell herself whenever her buttons get pushed by her mother.

◆

My mother is really getting to me. I have to remember that she is negative and tactless to all the other people in her life. Most of them have not put up with her. Mom is her own worst enemy and is pretty much alone now. I have chosen to stick by her, and, I guess, her tactless comments remain with her. It helps when I think of this as my mother posing a special challenge to me just like my boss at work, who is difficult to get along with. Maybe I can learn some ways to deal with them both that will serve me well in my life. I have to remember I don't have to accept my mother's invitation to fight her.

◆

This grownchild has learned to regard communicating with her mother as a challenge rather than a battle. Now she is ready to develop some skills to replace fighting—taking off her boxing gloves, so to speak—so she and her mother can preserve their relationship and not feel beaten up or beaten down by each other.

Here is an example of an exchange between a negative parent and a grownchild who has learned how to resist the fighting temptation. Imagine you are the grownchild and have just come over to visit your father.

◆

Your challenge is to deescalate and defuse your parent's negative comments.

DAD: The least you can do is pick me up some milk today.

DAUGHTER: Dad, we both arranged for it to be delivered— remember?

DAD: You have time for everyone but me. I suppose you are going to do errands for yourself today.

DAUGHTER: [just listens]

DAD: What's the matter? I suppose you don't like hearing the truth.

DAUGHTER: I'm listening to what you're saying and trying to put myself in your place.

Note that the daughter did not respond to her father's bait. She didn't make excuses for why she couldn't pick up the milk. If she had listed the reasons, it could have made things even worse by intensifying her father's feeling of unimportance. He might have responded with, "Oh, I'm not as important as your errands or your girlfriend . . ." or anyone or anything else she had mentioned. Keeping statements brief and empathizing are the key ingredients.

It isn't easy, but you can learn to deescalate and be less reactive. It takes practice. When clients come to us with problems like this, we often role-play with them. Try practicing this technique yourself with a close friend or family member. Stick to it. It's worth the effort.

Accentuate the Positive in Your Relationship with Your Parent

Perhaps you remember the old song about accentuating the positive and eliminating the negative. The writer of those lyrics didn't have negative parents in mind, but if your parent has a negative personality, take heed. There is a lot of wisdom in those words, because the key to having a positive relationship with your parent is to do things with her or for her that are least likely to bring out her negativity, and to avoid doing things that do. This tack will be best for both of you.

◆

Avoid the trap of doing things with and for your parent that are most likely to bring out her negativity. Pick activities that are most pleasurable for her and for you.

For some, that means being a son or daughter, not a caregiver. For example, there was one son who complained that whenever he tried to help his mother out by doing shopping for her, she found something to complain about. We advised him not to do shopping since that brings out the worst in her. Get someone else to do the shopping and other similar chores and relate to her in other ways. You and your negative parent have a long history together. Now that your parent's needs have increased with age, you are probably more involved. Don't be surprised if old buttons get pushed just as they did in adolescence with power struggles and distancing and whatever else went on at that time. However, now you and your parent don't have to rub up against each other as much. There is a whole outside world of resources that can dilute the tension. For example, you can hire private cab drivers to provide transportation, high school students to do errands, and homemaker helpers for companionship, driving, and cooking. You also can make use of such services as home-delivered groceries and home-delivered meals. And then this leaves you the time to do more pleasant things together. To find out about resources in your parents' locale, call the Eldercare Locator number 1-800-677-1116. This is a public service funded through the Administration on Aging.

For some families, it works best to come to see your parent with a specific activity in mind. Here are some examples that might just work with your parent.

- Balance her checkbook.
- Look at photographs and reminisce.
- Give her a manicure.
- Pick up a video on your way over and then watch it together.
- Take her out to a movie, a concert, or a play.
- Take her out to dinner.

Another piece of advice we give grownchildren in these situations is: Attend to yourself. Many grownchildren are so intent on focusing on what they can do to make their parent happier that they forget about attending to themselves. This dynamic also may have operated in their growing-up years. If so, it is helpful to identify any patterns and begin to make some changes so that you can be a happier person yourself.

◆

Keep up your own spirits. Try different things until you find what works.

Here are some comments of grownchildren that helped them to keep up their spirits all along the way.

"I get on the phone with my brother. He's the one person who knows how my mother can get to you. He can get me laughing when we reminisce."

"The thing that works best for me is pulling away for a while and writing in my journal."

"I get on the telephone with a good friend and she listens to my discouragement and then I feel bolstered."

"I get a couple of videos and spend the evening vegging out."

"I went out and bought myself a comforter to cuddle myself when I feel down."

"I get out and take a brisk walk. If the weather is bad, I get on my stationary bicycle."

◆

Keep your visits with a negative parent short.

More time with a negative parent is not always better. There is nothing you can do to make up for your parent's loneliness and misery, except to have steady contact with her. Long visiting periods make some people with these personality problems feel even more miserable and more alone when you leave. So when you visit your parent from out of town, try not to spend every moment with her. Rather than staying with your parent, consider staying at a hotel and planning some activities on your own in addition to visiting your parent.

◆

Try to keep from becoming negative yourself. Negativity is contagious.

You may find yourself buying in to your parent's despairing attitude that nothing will help. If you are becoming negative, this may be a warning signal that your own stress level is too high and that you need to give more attention to yourself and what you are going through. An excellent way to attend to yourself is to join a support group and/or get individual counseling. The important thing is to do whatever works for you to release tension and invigorate yourself so that your efforts will not drain you of energy and spirit.

When to Step in over Your Parent's Objection

There are no two ways about it: A parent's negativity can be stressful on the parent-grownchild relationship. But there are occasions when negativity can have graver consequences than simply fraying relationships between parents and grownchildren. If you think your parent's health and safety are at risk, and your parent's negativity keeps you from getting her some needed help, you must do more than be supportive and empathetic. That's when you have to step in.

The hard job is deciding whether the risk is high enough for you to intervene over your parent's objection with all the unpleasantness that is bound to occur. There are several factors that help you decide whether the risk is high enough to step in. You have to examine these risk factors as objectively and unemotionally as you can. If this is too hard for you, an outsider such as a geriatric care manager can help you with your objectivity.

The different risk situations in the following sections present examples that will serve as guidelines to help you make your own decisions.

High-Risk Situations

In this first situation, a mother is, like Elsie, recently widowed. But this woman's health is considerably worse than Elsie's. Here is what her daughter, Doris, had to say in one of our workshops.

◆

"I can't ever seem to be able to help my mother. Everything I suggest is 'no good.' She has always tended to be negative like this as far back as I can remember. I remember at least four friends she pushed away throughout her lifetime because she would make tactless and negative comments about their appearance or their children. Now she has no friends. It didn't matter so much before because she always had Dad. But my father died a year ago, and Mother is living alone in that old house of theirs. She is hanging on by the skin of her teeth.

"She skips dinner unless I sit with her. She has very high blood pressure, and it's critical that she take her pills regu-

larly. I can't tell whether she forgets to take them or uses it as an excuse for getting me to come over all the time. I also found burned pots under her kitchen cabinets. When I suggest that she take in a person to help care for the house and help her remember to take her pills, she refuses. I found a wonderful senior residence near my house where I know she would be well cared for. She said, 'Over my dead body.'

"I have reached the end of my rope."

◆

There are three risk factors in the situation Doris describes.

◆

You may have to override your parent's objection to outside help if the risk is too high.

• Her mother is skipping meals and losing weight.
• Her mother isn't taking her medications properly.
• Her mother is burning pots.

◆

When you decide to step in over a parent's objection, get the cooperation of family, friends, and outsiders.

These three factors were sufficiently indicative of a high-risk situation for Doris to step in despite her mother's objections. Her health was suffering, and she seemed a candidate for an accident at the stove or elsewhere. A good plan might be to hire a home helper to make meals, supervise medications, and offer companionship.

The next problem is how to step in. One way is for every family member to talk to the parent one-on-one. Another way is for the family to get together and meet with the parent to try to get her cooperation with accepting a helper or to come up with another acceptable plan of care. Sometimes a combination of the two methods is called for. There are some instances where the grownchildren know that no amount of convincing will work. In that circumstance, they just bring in the helper and hope that the parent accepts the help.

Such concerted action usually works if the family remains consistent. However, the results are often only temporary. For example, the mother might agree to a home helper, but after a few weeks become very angry at her family for intruding, fire the helper, and tell her children something like, "I'm not going to answer the door if she shows up tomorrow."

If nothing works or family members disagree over the level of risk involved, then the approach of last resort is to call in Adult Protective Services, a division of your local social services department. You may call the Eldercare Locator 1-800-677-1116 to get the telephone number of Adult Protective Services in your parents' locale. Doris or anyone concerned about her mother can make the call. By law, the caller's name will be kept confidential.

What happens then? A geriatric team, usually a nurse and a social worker, will respond and make a home visit to evaluate the risks and to determine what family supports are available. If Doris's mother is still unwilling to cooperate in an effort to remedy the situation, then it may well be advisable for a grownchild or other responsible person to take the legal steps to obtain guardianship where the court gives the right to make choices to her grownchild or some other responsible person. Usually, however, such extreme steps are not necessary. Most of the time, intervention by Adult Protective Services is enough to get people to cooperate.

◆

When intervention is necessary and all else fails, call Adult Protective Services.

Adult Protective Services workers do not strong-arm older adults into institutions. They try to work cooperatively with their clients and follow general principles, including:

- the client's right to self-determination. Competent adults are entitled to decide where and how they live.
- the use of the least restrictive alternative in treatment and placement.
- the use of community-based services rather than institutionalization, wherever possible.

Doris's mother remained resistant to her help. Still, Doris was not sure the situation was serious enough to call in Adult Protective Services. She was too angry to be able to see things objectively and she returned to us to review the alternatives. She realized her mother's safety was the most important consideration. Since her mother was closed off to all suggestions and was at serious risk from self-neglect, Doris was finally convinced that Adult Protective Services was the right way to go at this point.

It is relatively rare when a grownchild has to go to the extreme of calling in Adult Protective Services for help with a parent in a high-risk situation. In the following very common high-risk situation we were able to help a son, Joe, handle things on his own.

Joe described his problem at one of our support groups.

◆

"I'm scared to death my father is going to kill himself or some innocent victim with his driving. He drives twenty miles below the speed limit and makes turns from the middle lane. Sometimes he gets momentarily confused and just stops the car in the middle of the road.

"His vision is poor, his reaction time is slow, and sometimes he is disoriented. His doctor thinks this may be early Alzheimer's. Whenever I mention his driving, he gets red in the face and starts yelling, 'You're trying to rule my life and take away the last thing I can do.' I don't want to hurt him, but I don't want him to hurt himself or anyone else, either."

◆

"You're right to be scared to death," we told Joe. "It's obvious that an automobile accident is waiting to happen. But there are some other things that may not be so obvious to you. Your father said it all with his angry comment that you were trying to take away 'the last thing I can do.' This man is facing so many assaults to his mind and body, including poor vision and a slowing up of his physical and mental abilities. Then you and others are telling him he is not the same vigorous man that he was a few years earlier.

"The license to drive is symbolic of independence," we

continued. "Recall how you felt when you got your own license. It was a rite of transition into adulthood. Removing this privilege is traumatic for your father, and maybe for you, too. You have to empathize with him. Instead of thinking of this as a war of wills, think of it as a difficult situation for both of you."

Problems like this can happen to anyone, not simply to older people who have been negative all their lives. If you, like Joe, are having trouble getting your parent off the road, change your tactics. Help your parent save face. Don't yell at him that he has to stop driving. Talk to him calmly about

◆

Ally with your dad in difficult situations like having to stop driving.

Get a doctor to write a "no-driving" prescription.

how his vision isn't as good as it used to be. Remind him what his optometrist said the last time he went for an examination. If this doesn't work, enlist the aid of his doctor. One thing that often helps is for the doctor to write NO DRIVING on a prescription slip.

If more drastic action is called for, your state's Department of Motor Vehicles may be able to help. In some states a doctor's letter can initiate a license renewal examination before the old license has expired. If the state takes your parent's license away, then they are the bad guys, not you. That's the time when empathy can go a long way in helping your parent cope with this latest in a string of losses.

A LOW-RISK SITUATION
◆

Betty and her father, Ralph, are now living in the same city. Ralph had recently moved from North Carolina after the woman with whom he had been living for almost five years left him.

Ralph is in his early seventies and in good health. As Betty looked back on it, she realized that her father has always been dependent upon some woman or other. First it was her mother. Then, almost immediately after her death, he started going with a younger woman, who left him when his demands for her constant attention drove her away. Now, if he has his way, his daughter is to be the one to give him her full attention. Betty immediately finds herself spending ten hours a week doing things for her dad in addition to her full-time job and her two children. Of course it is not long before she is wearing herself out.

It is not only his never-ending demands that got to her but the fact that nothing she did for him was ever right. It brought back memories of her childhood when her father would come home from work and complain that his secretary (no matter who she happened to be at the time) could never do things right, and how her mother could never keep house quite to her father's satisfaction.

Her mother may have been willing to take it, but Betty is not. She knows there is no earthly reason why he cannot do more things for himself. She suggested to her father that he move into a senior apartment where there are many resources, including the opportunity to socialize.

Just as she feared, her father refused to move from his independent apartment to "a place with all those old people."

◆

It was then that Betty came to us for advice.

We can frame the advice we gave Betty in the form of a few questions and answers.

- Does your father have a right to stay in his apartment, even though it's not the best situation for you, his daughter? YES
- Are there risks in your father's situation that warrant your trying to force him to move when he doesn't want to? NO
- Should you back off? YES
- If you don't want to continue your role as caregiver, are there other options for you? YES

Betty's dad has the right to decide how he lives, even if it looks to everyone else that there is a better way. Unless there are risks of self-neglect or self-abuse, no intervention is indicated.

But that does not mean Betty has to play by his rules. Even though she can't force him to move, she should recognize there are other ways of helping her father while, at the same time, relieving the stress on herself. One thing she can do is see what her community has to offer in the way of services for seniors. She can provide him with this information and, if he agrees, she can make arrangements for services such as home-delivered meals, and errand and transportation services.

♦

If the risk is low, back off. It isn't worth the aggravation of a power struggle.

When you evaluate your situation and discover that the risks are relatively low, then back off. At the same time provide ideas and resource information to a receptive parent.

Moderate Risk . . . Getting a Foot in the Door

Not all situations are black and white. In fact, there are many gray situations where there is potentially some risk involved.

Judy describes her father's situation in this way.

♦

I have stayed away from Dad for the last ten years because he does bad things for my self-esteem. When I was younger, he would yell at me for nothing, especially when he was drunk. He was fired many times for his hostility toward his bosses. His kid brother never calls him. There's really no one left in his life. I came back when I got a letter from his neighbor saying he was losing his memory and that he shouldn't be left alone.

There are roaches in the kitchen sink along with dirty dishes, not much in the refrigerator, and what there is looks stale. He's more drawn into himself and more irritable than ever. I told Dad he had to accept a housekeeper who could make his meals and clean up the house. He blamed me for upsetting his routine. He would not hear of any stranger coming into the house.

◆

Judy might try seeking the help of a neutral party such as a geriatric care manager, a professional who can objectively evaluate the situation. The care manager will first of all try to get her foot in the door and then establish a relationship with Judy's father on the basis of whatever service need he acknowledges. For example, if he says he has trouble with shopping and cooking, then the care manager can ally with him to solve this problem. Sometimes a person such as Judy's father will allow an outsider into his world in preference to his own family.

◆

If you are not sure whether to step in, step back and get your bearings.

You might be too close to your parent's situation to be objective.

If so, hire a neutral third party—a care manager—to weigh the risks and advise you.

At the same time the care manager is attending to the practical matter of seeing that Judy's dad eats properly, she will begin to make an assessment of his memory difficulty and to observe how capable he is of functioning independently. She will help Judy view her father's situation more objectively, and will discuss the level of risk involved here along with planning the next steps, if any. She can also help the family by providing some insights into his lifelong difficult personality.

It may be that the only risk at this time is the fact that Judy's father may eat stale or rotting food. If that is the case, she might simply check his refrigerator regularly for old food and supplant it with fresh food. When a parent is hostile, it is easier to do a specific task as just described rather than come up with a more radical plan of care. Doing what's acceptable is often the wisest approach.

When to Step In

In all three risk scenarios, the grownchildren of negative parents were at the end of their ropes. Each wanted to step in and help her parent, but her efforts were flatly rejected. Many grownchildren in these situations see things in one extreme or the other: They believe they have to force their parent to accept help, or that they will have to pull out of the situation entirely.

We suggest another alternative: Step back, get your bearings, and evaluate the relative risks in your situation using the guidelines at your right. The moderate-risk situation, such as the one just described, is the most difficult to evaluate because it deals with gray areas. If you feel stuck, then consider a consultation with a geriatric care manager to help you assess your parent's risk factors. In this way you can also gain a more objective perspective of what makes your parent tick and why he or she is so resistant to change.

◆

Evaluate the risk to your parent's safety. If the risk is high, step in; if not, step back.

If you can't evaluate the risk, get professional help.

If you do step in, get family members to talk to your parent one-on-one, or, have a family planning meeting with the parent.

If your parent is closed to all discussion and reasoning, try bringing in someone to help with a specific task, such as food shopping.

As a last resort, call in Adult Protective Services.

Why Do Difficult Parents Resist So Much?

Most people pride themselves on their independent spirits and self-directed lives. Older people are no different. They might be inclined to disagree with some of their children's ideas or opinions, just as you may be with your own children or friends. You have your way of doing things and don't want to be told what to do or how to do it.

Sometimes an older person's resistance to a grownchild's

ideas can be a healthy refusal to give in to the demands of others. It may be that the son or daughter is too insistent in trying to change a parent's lifestyle out of the feeling that he knows better and his parent ultimately will be happier following his advice.

The easiest way to understand this is to imagine yourself as an older person, perhaps in your eighties or even older. You may be suffering several losses, including sight or hearing, energy, and mobility, but at the same time adjusting as best you can. Sure, you have slowed down a bit. And then along come your children implying that you are not doing "it" right—that they know better. You might well be annoyed. Isn't it difficult enough adjusting to these losses? Must you also have to put up with "know-it-all" children? However, after some thought, you may well come to your own conclusion that certain changes have to be made for your own health and safety, and you adapt as best you can.

Now put yourself in the position of someone like Doris's mother in the earlier example. All your life you have been coping with depression. You have built up a set of rigid defenses to protect you from depression and have always resisted any changes that might weaken those defenses. Now you are older and in poor health, and along come your children trying to convince you that some big changes in lifestyle are necessary. Just the thought of making a change makes you anxious. You are surely going to dig in your heels and resist those changes with all your strength.

◆

Difficult parents are especially resistant to change because change can erode their lifelong defenses.

Healthy aging requires an adaptive way of thinking about oneself—I can't do such and such, but I'll find another way. This isn't easy for anyone. But those who have been difficult all their lives have a still harder time accepting the losses of aging. Their difficulties in coping with aging go beyond normal resistance. Aging poses a special threat to their equilibrium. Thus Doris's mother found it impossible to adapt to her changed situation. Her inflexibility got in the way of sensible decision making. For her to recognize she was having trouble managing on her own was to admit complete defeat.

The Critical Person

If you have a negative parent similar to any of those in the preceding examples, then you know that negativity almost never occurs by itself—these turnoff behaviors usually come in bunches. You know, for example, that if your mother is so negative, she resists every suggestion you make, she probably criticizes you for making them and may well act in a hostile and suspicious manner toward you. So intermingled are these behaviors that the one often blends into the other.

A critical parent is very hard to take. You well know it is natural to want to defend yourself against an attack or to counterattack. If you do this, your parent invariably will escalate the attack, and you may escalate it still more. This is a contest in which no one wins. Both of you feel angrier and more hurt by the end of such an exchange.

Don't respond to your parent in kind. It doesn't work. Instead, learn to react to her criticism with a new nondefensive, noncritical strategy. The next time your parent criticizes you for something, take a deep breath and let her criticisms roll off your back. Isn't it hard to respond in one way after a lifetime of responding in another? You can do it once you understand why your parent feels so compelled to criticize. These criticisms are a projection of her own profound sense of inadequacy. She gets rid of these feelings by convincing herself that those around her have worse imperfections. So she engages in one-upmanship, in which she puts others down—especially those closest to her. This is how she copes with her world. And when you get defensive, her feelings of inadequacy are intensified. It follows that if you ride with the punches and

◆

Understand that your parent's criticisms are deeply embedded in her personality. Respond with understanding, not defensiveness.

don't criticize back, then she will be more confident and let up on you a bit.

One thing that helps is to expect the worst: Assume that every time you are together, your parent will make some kind of critical remark. Then create some scenarios based on your past experience in which she criticizes you, and think about how you might react. For example, imagine that you went to visit her and she greeted you with, "That necktie looks terrible with your suit. Are you color-blind or something?" In the past you might have responded with, "I don't know what you are talking about. I think the tie looks perfectly fine." Instead, you might say, "Maybe you're right, Mother. I'll have to get a better light for my bedroom."

Another approach is to deflect the criticism. For example, here is how a client of ours was greeted by her mother one day: "Honey, where did you get those shoes? They are awful looking."

Instead of personalizing the remark and getting angry, as in the past, our client was prepared for the attack and deflected it by saying, "Oh, I don't know, Mom, I like the shoes *you* are wearing. Where did you get them?"

Her mother responded with, "You like them? Remember that weekend when your father and I went away to the beach, I found them at that cute little shop . . ."

Responding as she did, our client turned the focus of the conversation from herself to her mother, in an area in which she shines.

Think up situations in which you can expect to be criticized, and some benign responses for each. It is sometimes helpful to practice your responses by role-playing with someone else.

What can be even worse than your being criticized is when your parent needs the help of others and then proceeds to turn her helper off with criticism. This was the case with one of our clients, Beth, who told us about how Molly, her mother-in-law, was constantly criticizing Elaine, her helper.

◆

Here is what she said to me when I visited her one day:
"That woman is so fat. No wonder. All she ever does is eat

and watch television." Molly didn't whisper those words. She practically shouted them out. I could have fallen through the floor. Elaine couldn't help but hear her. And this probably wasn't the first time Molly said hurtful things in front of Elaine. "Why do you talk that way, Mother?" I responded. "You know how much she does for you. She is going to leave if you keep on behaving this way."

"Good riddance," was the angry reply.

◆

Beth couldn't imagine how Elaine would stay with this insulting boss. Elaine's services were essential. Molly was a diabetic, and Elaine was hired to give her a hand with housekeeping, shopping, and cooking when her son discovered that his mother was forgetting to follow her diet.

Beth's husband explained that as far back as he could remember, his mother had always been negative and critical. The result was predictable: She had no friends and had managed to alienate just about everyone in her family. But now it was more than alienating family members. If Molly couldn't keep a helper, her health was at risk. Could anything be done about this lifelong behavior?

We pointed out to Beth that there were things she and her husband could do to cope with her mother-in-law's critical behavior. The most important thing was to understand that Molly does not have the inner control that most people have to censor her thoughts. When under stress, whatever comes into her mind is likely to come out of her mouth. People like Molly who struggle with problems of self-image, with a lack of judgment, and with weak self-control have a particularly difficult time with the aging process. The normal losses of aging, such as short-term memory loss, are unacceptable flaws. Instead of accepting responsibility for what she perceived as her own shortcomings, she finds fault in others.

Critical people like Molly often don't even realize that they are being critical—they don't have the emotional capability to understand this. Nor do they have the capacity to realize how

the helper feels about the criticism. So don't defend the helper—
that would only make your parent angry at you and even more
critical of the helper. Instead, try to convince your parent that criticizing a helper is unwise because it can turn the helper against her,
and that it is in her interest to be nice to
her so that she will go out of her way to
do nice things for her boss in return.

◆

When your parent
criticizes a helper:
• tell your parent how
her criticism can backfire.
• don't defend the helper
to your mother.
• shore up the helper.

In addition to working on your parent, try to shore up the helper. Take
her aside and explain to her that your
parent can't help behaving this way,
that she has had this problem all her
life, and that she is her own worst
enemy. Praise her often and show your
appreciation for her patience and dedication. Rather than taking the criticism personally, someone like Elaine may sympathize with her employer once she realizes how miserable the
older woman feels and that she is unable to control herself.

The Suspicious Parent

We have seen how negativity and criticalness can be intensified
in older people as the normal assaults of aging take their toll.
The same is also true of suspicion, another in our list of turnoff
behaviors. It's easy to understand how a person who has been
suspicious all her life can become even more so, even to the
point of paranoia in the face of the memory problems that
often occur in the later years.

Here is how one daughter described her mother.

◆

*"Mother always took her diamond ring off and placed it
on the kitchen counter when she did the dishes. Today, the
housekeeper was coming, so she hid the ring inside the
kitchen cabinet. When the housekeeper left, Mother couldn't
find her ring. It wasn't in the usual places—either on the*

kitchen counter or in her jewelry box in her dresser drawer. She jumped to conclusions, and the following dialogue ensued.

MOTHER: *"Mindy [the housekeeper] stole my diamond ring."*

DAUGHTER: *"You sound very upset. Try to calm down and remember where you put it."*

MOTHER: *"I remember exactly where I put it! There's nothing wrong with my memory! You're always taking the other person's side."*

DAUGHTER: *"I'm just asking you to use your good sense and stop accusing Mindy. She's never taken anything from you in twenty years."*

MOTHER: *"I don't care whether you believe me or not. She stole my ring, and I'm going to go over to her house and ask for it back."*

DAUGHTER: *"Mother, that's not a very smart thing to do."*

The mother is reacting defensively to her daughter's patronizing remarks. People with this lifelong personality get frightened when anyone insinuates that something is wrong with their memory. This gets interpreted as something wrong with their mind, and with being crazy.

As you can imagine, this situation escalated into an unpleasant scene. The mother was clearly mistrustful about Mindy, the housekeeper, and truly believed that she had stolen her ring. Once a person has paranoid thoughts, it is impossible to be rational with her. The tension only increases in this scenario where the daughter tries to point out the realities to her mother.

◆

You can't talk your parent out of being suspicious. But you can support whatever she is feeling, whether she is scared, unsettled, or upset.

Here is an example of a more effective way of dealing with the situation. In this dialogue, the daughter validates her mother's feelings rather than attacking her beliefs.

MOTHER: *"Mindy stole my diamond ring."*

DAUGHTER: *"That's upsetting."*

MOTHER: *"Yes. I'm going over to her house and getting it back. Will you drive me over?"*

DAUGHTER: *"I won't have time now because I have to prepare dinner. Meanwhile, I'll be thinking about what to do about your ring. Tell me exactly how this happened. Was anyone else in the house? When did you discover it? Was anything else taken?"*

In this dialogue, the daughter did not argue with her mother's accusation that Mindy had stolen her ring. She empathized with her mother's upset reaction. Remember, you cannot talk your parent out of a paranoid belief. What you can do is sympathize, with phrases such as, "I'd be upset, too," or, "That's terrible!"

You may hesitate to use these sympathetic phrases because it may sound like you are encouraging your parent's paranoid beliefs. On the contrary, your parent feels frightened and needs to feel that you are on her side. Comments such as these will have a quieting and comforting effect. Don't underestimate their importance.

Notice how the daughter asked questions about the specifics. Sticking to a factual discussion is more constructive and less threatening than the previous role play where the daughter tried to use the no-win tactic of reasoning.

Of course there is always the possibility that your parent's suspiciousness is so all-pervasive that it severely limits her day-to-day functioning. If this happens with your parent, see a psychiatrist who is experienced with older people. It may be that medication is indicated, particularly if delusions or hallucinations are present.

Discovering the Cause of Later-Life Turnoff Behaviors

Turnoff behaviors, as with any of the other difficult behaviors, can show up for the first time later in life. Here is how Nancy described her problem with her father.

"Ever since my mother died three years ago, I have been able to keep my ninety-year-old father at home by hiring full-time housekeepers to stay with him. Over time he has become more and more critical of these helpers, sometimes to the point of nastiness. He was never like this before. I'm getting to the point where I can't keep helpers anymore. I can't think of any reason for this personality change in my dad. Maybe this sort of thing just happens to people when they get older.

◆

We assured Nancy that people don't just get nasty or anything else when they get old. There has to be a reason, and it's important that we find it because once we do, we may be able to figure out a way of reversing the nastiness. Recall the examples of later-life dependency in Chapter 1, where the grownchildren worked patiently with their parents to restore them to their old selves.

◆

Personality changes don't occur in old age without a cause.

It's worth the effort to find the reason.

Then you'll be in a better position to do something about reversing it.

Sometimes the reasons for the personality change are evident. This was not so in Nancy's situation, and it may not be in yours. The source of the difficulties can be physical or emotional. The approach we suggested to Nancy was to look for physical reasons and if these are ruled out, then look for emotional reasons. Here is the set of questions that we posed to Nancy to get at possible physical causes.

- When was your father's last general checkup? Is he in any physical discomfort?
- Is his memory getting worse? If so, have him checked out by his doctor. It is common for a person to feel a loss of control with the realization that he is becoming less mentally alert. This sometimes comes out as anger and irritability.
- Have his medications changed? When was the last time

a physician reviewed them knowing the history of his behavioral changes?

• Is he taking his medications properly?
• Is he eating properly?

If none of these questions give you a clue, think about emotional reasons for his behavior changes. For instance, your dad still may be grieving your mom's death.

If the detective in you finds out the major culprit is emotional, then we suggest that you and your siblings have serious talks with your parent. Share your observations and concerns with him and see what light he can shed on the matter. Figure out together what measures might be taken to relieve his upset. If he is not cooperative, then you have to deal with the realities of the way he is behaving. You may have to take a direct approach and spell out acceptable and unacceptable behaviors.

We suggested that Nancy consider finding a care manager who would supervise the situation at home. Such an outsider is usually more effective than a grownchild in mediating between a helper and the older person. Let the professional evaluate how much home care your dad really needs. Sometimes grownchildren impose too much care and take over in areas that are not necessary.

The Overwhelming Loneliness of People with Turnoff Behaviors

If you were confronted with a person who turned hot and cold on you, criticized you, suspected your motives, and resisted every suggestion you made, then you would want as little as possible to do with that person. That is why such people are typically friendless. Children, too, are driven away only to return later when the parent needs help, more out of a sense of guilt or responsibility than love.

But remember that as bad as she makes others feel, she feels still worse and she can't run away from herself. So she remains alone with herself and her inner torment.

The most effective thing that a grownchild can do for himself and for his parent is to learn why she behaves as she does. Understanding almost always leads to empathy, and this is the first step to making progress of any kind. Even a small change in the way you react to your parent can make a big difference in the way she reacts to you and others around her.

◆

If you understand why your parent turns people off, you will treat her differently. Even a small shift by you can make a big difference in her.

4

SELF-CENTERED BEHAVIORS

> ### SELF-CENTERED BEHAVIORS
>
> #### When your parent:
>
> ◆ has a distorted self-image, viewing self as "something special" at one end, or inadequate at the other.
> ◆ interprets events solely as to how they affect him or her, oblivious to the effect on others.
> ◆ is insensitive to the needs of others while, at the same time, thinks of self as generous.
> ◆ guards his or her own turf.
> ◆ is jealous of others.
> ◆ is preoccupied with physical problems, real or imagined.

As our parents get older and experience the various impairments that come with the aging process, we expect them to focus more on themselves than in their earlier years. But what about the person who has always felt the need to be the center of attention and has behaved in ways that she thinks will assure this? If your parent is like this, chances are that she has been a source of irritation or aggravation as long as you can remember. You may have tried to distance yourself from your parent as much as you could. But now that your parent is experiencing the problems of aging, she is even more self-centered and she needs you more than ever.

A VAIN MOTHER WON'T ACCEPT HELP

Here is an example, typical of many that we see every day in our practice. Marge came to us looking for another place for her mother, Gert, to live, one in which her mother might be safer and get some supervision. This is the way she put it.

◆

My mother's health and vision have been failing steadily during the last couple of years. But she is so hard to help. She talks like she is a fifty-year-old who can go anywhere she likes anytime she likes. But she acts like an invalid who won't make the effort to do anything on her own. She waits for me on Saturdays, my only day off, to answer her mail and to take her everywhere.

Whenever I suggest a move, she gets angry at me. She broke her hip a few months ago. She is unsteady on her feet and has fallen twice in recent weeks. Still, she refuses to use her walker or even a cane when she goes out. "Everyone will think I am a cripple," she says.

Mother has always been vain like this. But "vain" is a mild word to use in describing my mother. She has never hesitated to brag about her talents and to take credit for my success as well. What's more, she hasn't a clue as to how I think or feel about anything. It's her opinion, and hers only, that counts. She assumes that I think as she does.

My sister, Shirley, summed it up beautifully. "She is the sun and everyone else near her is a planet orbiting around her." It reminded me of the story of Joseph in the book of Genesis, who dreamed that his father, mother, and all his brothers bowed down to him. In the story Joseph's brothers paid him back for his egotism. Shirley and I never thought of paying Mother back, but both of us escaped her clutches by marrying early and moving away.

Of course, even though I now live near her, she never lets me forget that I once "deserted" her. Now that she really needs more attention, my sister and I find her demands exasperating, yet we are her daughters and feel responsible and obliged to make sure she's okay. She has treated both our husbands like intruders to be ignored. Of course she would deny this. I consider myself lucky that our marriage hasn't been damaged by Mother's impossible demands for my exclusive attention.

◆

How Narcissistic People Typically Behave

The word commonly used to describe Gert's behavior is "narcissistic." The term comes from Narcissus, a character in Greek mythology, who fell in love with his own reflection. People use it in ordinary discourse to mean a person with an inflated sense of himself or herself. And this definition seemed to fit Gert, at least through the eyes of her daughter.

When we use the word "narcissistic," we're not referring to a healthy sense of self-worth. We would not describe a woman who takes pride in her ability to bring up a child or hold a job as narcissistic.

◆

A narcissistic person needs constant propping up to feel good about himself.

But Gert is different. Her feeling of grandiosity has been lifelong and is so extreme that her daughters certainly would not call it healthy. What is the difference?

The essential difference between healthy pride and unhealthy narcissism has to do with whether or not the person's self-esteem is internally based or dependent on praise and recognition from others. When a person with a healthy sense of self-worth accomplishes something, be it small or large, he takes satisfaction for his accomplishment within himself. He certainly enjoys having others praise him for what he has done, but he doesn't require this praise to feel good about himself. On the other hand, the person with unhealthy narcissism cannot take satisfaction in his accomplishments without the adulation of those around him. Take the example of a world-renowned mathematician, a professor at a major university for many years. A typical professor in his position would have had dozens of Ph.D. students during his long career. This man had very few, because he quickly became known for taking the credit for his students' accomplishments. Here was a man who already had a great reputation for his own legitimate accomplishments but who kept stealing the work of his students to keep the adulation fires burning.

Gert is, like the professor, hungry for adulation. It makes no difference that she has ordinary talents and he had extraordinary ones. The internal mechanism is the same. Each requires constant propping up by those around them.

Oftentimes, people with extreme or unhealthy narcissism lead successful and sometimes prominent lives as long as they can structure their environment so that they constantly receive admiration and adulation to boost their feelings of worth. They are preoccupied with their own beauty, power, and success, having little capacity for empathy toward others. Since right underneath this inflated exterior lies a vulnerable and hypersensitive self, they easily feel the deep emotional wounds when criticized.

♦

Underneath the inflated ego lies a vulnerable and hypersensitive self.

You can get a good idea of the ways in which unhealthy narcissism shows up by taking a closer look at some of the statements in Marge's story about her mother.

"Everyone will think I'm a cripple [if I use the cane]." When Gert fell and broke her hip, it was a tremendous blow to her identity as a beautiful woman. We learned that all her life she would spend hours and hours primping in front of the mirror before going to a dinner party. She always befriended much younger people, needing to see herself as young and vital. With such an attitude, it is no wonder she has had a hard time adapting to her own aging. The whole idea of using a cane would make her feel very old and ugly inside and out.

"She never hesitated to brag about her talents and take credit for my success as well." Gert has a grandiose sense of specialness that inflates her ego and keeps herself boosted in her eyes and before others. This grandiosity makes up for feelings of inferiority and worthlessness. She sees her daughter, Marge, as an extension of her rather than a separate person. Years ago when Marge would bring in first prize for a painting in grade school, her mother would feel as if it were she who had won, or that it was to her credit her daughter was so talented.

"She hasn't a clue as to how I think or feel about anything. It's her opinion that counts. She assumes that I think as she does." This woman has a limited capacity for empathy and a kind of indifference toward the needs of others, including her own daughter. In plainer language, she cannot feel the pain or happiness or disappointment for her daughter, so she can never really get to know her. Children such as Marge generally feel quite emotionally distant from their parent.

◆

Narcissistic people are typically unempathic, controlling, and opinionated.

This mother also tends to be very controlling as a way of preserving her false feelings of superiority. She has to control her environment and the people around her rather than bear the uncomfortable emotions that may arise without such control. Extremely narcissistic people tend to feel their opinion is right and the one that counts. They devalue those who disagree with them.

"She has treated both our husbands like intruders to be ignored." Gert wants exclusive attention from her daughters. She wants them to cater to her, admire her, and behave like planets rotating around her. Therefore she is jealous of others who pull her planets away from her as if they are intruders. Rather than enjoy an expanded family, she, like other extremely narcissistic people, wants her daughters to attend to her alone and to no one else. This can result in a lot of family strife.

Getting Along with a Narcissistic Parent Without Wearing Out

Marge's problem with her narcissistic mother is hardly unique. Perhaps you are in a similar quandary as to how to handle your parent. The first step to preserving your relationship with your parent is to understand that these narcissistic characteristics are deeply ingrained in her personality. So instead of wearing yourself out by trying to get her to change, focus on changing your own attitudes and behavior.

You can't fix your mother any more than Marge could fix hers. Sometimes a grownchild in this situation will put his life on hold trying to satisfy his parent's needs above his own. There is no satiation point. What helps is giving up the

> ◆
>
> It helps when you give up futile attempts to try to satisfy your narcissistic parent.

fantasy of ever succeeding in making your parent feel good in a sustained way. Then you will be able to refocus your energies more constructively and have greater tolerance for your parent.

Don't fall into Marge's trap of behaving like her controlling mother by trying to force her to do what she doesn't want to do, i.e., move to an-

> ◆
>
> Stop power struggles.

other living situation. The power struggle that resulted got both mother and daughter angry and caused the two of them to distance themselves from each other emotionally.

Once you understand how extremely narcissistic people behave and how you react to your own narcissistic parent, you will be on your way to becoming more sympathetic and less angry with your parent. If your mother is like Marge's, you will learn that even though she needs catering to (grocery shopping, sorting through mail, compan-

> ◆
>
> Avoid situations that put you in conflict with your parent. Get others to help, and spend your time in less conflictual activities.

ionship), you and your siblings don't have to do it all. Who else is there? Here is a list of other kinds of helpers from both formal and informal support systems who can help an older person stay in her home and increase her safety and self-reliance.

- a geriatric care manager to coordinate a network of helpers and recommend meaningful activities for your parent (inside and outside the home)

- high school students in the neighborhood to do errands
- a home health worker who drives
- a physical therapist to make a home visit, evaluate her unsteadiness, and make recommendations
- other family members to visit on a regular schedule
- friends of the family to visit
- volunteers from the church or synagogue to visit

◆

Make it clear what you can and cannot do, in a constructive and nonthreatening way.

And make sure the timing is right.

Tell your parent clearly what you can do and what others can do. Introducing other people into Gert's narrowing world can be very difficult. But remember that it matters *how* you do it. There are both threatening and nonthreatening ways.

The worst thing Marge can do is blurt out the idea of introducing a helper in the heat of anger, as for example: "Mom, I can't stand to come over here and be your servant. I quit. I'm going to find someone else."

Marge can have a much better chance of succeeding by introducing the idea of a helper with a calm and reassuring approach. But first she has to decide what to say and how to say it. Marge came to the conclusion she could no longer spend all day Saturday with her mother. Her pattern was to come early in the morning, take care of all kinds of practical chores, and later in the day take her mother out. The solution was to get someone else to help with the practical chores, and she would use her time on things that were more pleasant for both of them. One of these unpleasant chores was helping with the mail, because it often led to arguments between the two of them. Here is how she handled it.

"Mom, I know you are used to my sorting through your mail every Saturday. I'm going to have Haley, that pretty sixteen-year-old girl from down the street, help out with the mail. I'll still be coming every Saturday, but with Haley's help, we will be able to spend more fun time together visiting or going out. I'll see you next Saturday."

It was important for Marge to assure her mother that she

will be coming back Saturday to keep her from feeling wounded at the idea of her daughter hiring a high school girl as a replacement for herself. It is also important for Marge to pick the right time to say it—a time when Marge feels rational and calm, not angry and resentful.

Now many of you probably are saying to yourself that your mother would never agree to this kind of deal. She would need a reason for such a radical change of routine. Here is an example of how another daughter introduced the idea of bringing in a helper because her health was suffering.

MOTHER: Don't forget to come at nine tomorrow. I have a dentist appointment and then several errands to do.

DAUGHTER: Mom, I won't be able to take you. I'm coming over at eight in the morning to introduce you to Susie, who will take you and bring you back. She will make your lunch and leave at about noon.

MOTHER: *[interrupting]* Honey, that will not work. No one else is going to sit around the house, have lunch with me, and watch the soaps.

DAUGHTER: I'm going to have to ask you to try it. I went to my doctor the other day and she told me she was concerned about my blood pressure and that I have to take better care of myself and get more rest. What I want to do is have more relaxing time with you. So I'll see you tomorrow morning to introduce you to Susie and then I'll be over on Sunday for our usual brunch, Mom.

MOTHER: Who is this Susie?

Here the daughter was direct about her health problems, but calm and reassuring at the same time. Even a very self-centered parent may respond to a grownchild's health problem, if only out of fear that she would be in real trouble without her. One of the biggest challenges for grownchildren is to set limits for themselves about what they can and cannot do for their parent. Setting limits is so hard because of deep feelings that their parents were there for them when they were growing up, so they feel they need to be there for them. But parents who are dependent or very self-centered can be so unreasonably demanding that their children have to set limits for their own emotional and physical health.

The bottom line here is that a very self-centered parent has a never-satisfied need for being bolstered and attended to, which requires some of your attention but not so much that it interferes with your own health or general well-being.

Telling a Parent She Can't Live with You

"Mom wants to move out of her home and come live with us in our house. It would be a catastrophe." This was the dilemma facing Amy when she came to us for help. Amy's mother was, in her own words, "perfect." "If I had to live my life over again, I would do everything exactly the same," was something she said over and over again. Amy's mother would come for a visit once or twice a year from her home in Florida. These visits were difficult but tolerable because they never lasted more than a few days. But this visit was different. For the first time, the older woman told her daughter of her heart condition, which led her to make the request to live with her daughter.

Older parents often desire to live with their children, and there are many reasons why. For one thing, there is the old tradition of multiple generations living under one roof. This was the norm in generations past. Indeed, there were few available alternatives. Another common reason is loneliness. A widowed parent seeks comfort from her children and grandchildren in preference to living alone or with "strangers" in some setting.

Amy's mother may have had one or both of these reasons in mind when she made her request, but she was most likely driven by her narcissistic personality. It was a blow to her ego to learn that even she, a "perfect" person, had a heart problem. Being close to her daughter was a way to be sure that her daughter would continue to love her despite her physical shortcomings.

Some grownchildren are agreeable to having a parent or

even a grandparent move in. We have seen instances where a grownchild will go to great expense to remodel her home to cater to the needs of a physically disabled parent. But when the parent has a difficult personality, the natural reaction of the grownchild is almost always like Amy's: She has to find a way to keep her mother from moving in with her.

Making the decision not to have your parent move in is hard, but telling a parent, even a difficult one, is even harder. It is the ultimate in limit setting. But no matter what your circumstances are, there is a tactful way of discussing this delicate issue with your parent.

We have found it helpful in situations like this to keep the following principles in mind.

- Be as honest as possible while helping your parent save face.
- Always be kind and considerate.
- Assure your parent that even though she can't live with you, you nevertheless care about her.
- Be straightforward. Open up a discussion if your parent is hinting around about wanting to move in with you.
- Don't be defensive. Defensive explanations always lead to counterdefensive arguments.
- Listen and respect your parent's reactions while you are persistent and clear about your position.

After her counseling sessions, Amy talked things over with her sister and husband. Then she had a conversation with her mother that went as follows.

AMY: I'm glad you're thinking it's not wise to live so far away now that your health is so shaky. Sis and I are relieved that you are willing to move back here. Ben and I appreciate your offer to improve our house. But we just don't think it will work out. You know how you and I irritate

each other. We just don't see eye to eye on so many things.
It will be better for both of us if there is some space
between us.

MOTHER: You'll have plenty of privacy with the new addition
that I'll build for you, and I'll be able to help with the
children.

AMY: Mom, we've thought it out carefully. It will work out
best if you live nearby.

Amy remained honest and positive throughout this delicate
dialogue. First she supported her mother coming to live nearby
because of her failing health. Then she was honest in confronting
their past difficulties. She avoided lengthy defensive explanations
that easily might have escalated into an angry argument. And
finally she remained firm when her mother began to insist.

◆

Tailor your approach
to your own situation
in finding a way to
answer your parent's
request to live with
you.

But think carefully
about how you do it.

The approach you take with your
parent depends on the particulars of
the situation. There may be some aspects of your own situation that can
help you find the right words, provided
you are thoughtful and considerate
about it. Here are a few examples.

• **For a mother who is hinting
by telling stories of how
other "good" daughters open
their homes to their mothers.**
Mom, I'd like to be like Sophie's daughter, but you and
I know I'm not like her. I tend to get irritable and short-
tempered when I don't have my way or my space. It's
never worked when we are together for too long. We
will both be happier living in separate places.

• **For a couple with a newly emptied nest.** As you
know, Ben and I have just sent our last kid off to college.
It's important for the two of us to be alone in our own
home now. But Ben and I would love to have you
nearby.

• **For a single parent or grownchild living alone.**
Mom, you know how we rub each other the wrong way

when we are together too much. I would like to have the best of both worlds, where I have my own home and you live close enough so we can get together often.

- **For parents of teenagers.** Mom, you know as well as I that the kids are very difficult at this age. It would be hard for all of us to live together.

- **For a father who feels he can ease the family's financial problems by contributing rent.** Dad, it's more important to stay good friends by living separately and close by. You know how we do better when we aren't under the same roof. It will be great to have you nearby.

Whether or not there is a special situation similar to one of the preceding, it is important to be firm about what you can and cannot do and, at the same time, be kind and considerate.

The Mother-in-law Who Came to "Help"

Don't think that only narcissistic people are self-centered. There are people who are self-effacing and dependent—nothing at all like the grandiose persons we have been talking about—who also can be very self-centered. Remember Rose in Chapter 1, who got sick whenever her son planned a vacation. People such as Rose are so emotionally needy that they are all absorbed in seeing to it that everyone around them caters to them. On the surface, a person such as Rose with a deflated sense of herself, and one such as Gert, the mother at the beginning of this chapter with an inflated sense of herself, appear to be as different as can be. But underneath they are both hypersensitive and fearful of depressive aloneness, rejection, and abandonment, and they often behave in similar ways. Here is an example.

◆

Norma and Jim came to our offices for help in dealing with Jim's mother, Kate. Norma had given birth to their first child a few weeks before, and Kate had offered to come help. They appreciated the offer, but were hesitant to accept. Kate had always been so sensitive and hard to get along with. They recalled her visit three years ago to spend Thanksgiving with them. They were all invited out to dinner, and Norma baked a beautiful pumpkin pie for dessert. When the three of them arrived at their friends' home, Norma was carrying the pie. But, as she stepped inside the house, she slipped on the threshold and dropped the pie. She immediately bent down and tried to retrieve as much of the dessert as she could. It was a horrible experience.

But not nearly as horrible as the ride home after dinner. As soon as they got in the car, Kate became very cold and uncommunicative, finally blurting out, "I have never been so humiliated in all my life. You did not introduce me to our hosts. You treated me like a servant girl." In the panic over the dropped pie, both Norma and Jim had been so absorbed in picking up the ill-fated dessert that they had neglected the formality of introductions. Of course, they all had chatted amiably during dinner, and the hosts were very solicitous toward their guest. But it wasn't enough for Kate. She was devastated by this perceived slight. Norma told us how put out she was. "It never occurred to her that she should be concerned about how bad I must have felt about the ruined dessert."

Despite this experience, Kate's offer seemed so genuine that they put aside their old feelings and welcomed her visit. "She arrived just after lunch, wearing her best black suit with a pretty white blouse. I was nursing the baby. Kate sat there and commented, 'I don't think you have enough milk, dear.' I had so much milk that Jimmy doubled his birth weight in only two months."

"These words didn't exactly encourage me, but I was hopeful that things would settle down. Later in the afternoon, Kate was still wearing that black suit and made no effort to help with dinner. The next morning she came down in the same black suit and expected me to make her breakfast. After a week of this, Jim and I were ready to hire a helper

to help, not with the baby but with Kate. One morning, I didn't make breakfast for Kate. She, in her black suit, had to do it herself. Within a few hours she was on her way home. She hasn't talked to us since then. I guess she really felt hurt and rejected."

◆

Kate had good intentions. Her offer to travel five hundred miles to be with her new grandchild showed this. Helping with the new baby was as beyond her capacity now, as was overlooking her daughter-in-law's perceived Thanksgiving Day slight three years ago. She is all absorbed in herself. It is the only way she can cope with her deep feelings of insecurity. She is the same person she was at that Thanksgiving Day incident. She has been like that all her life and, in all likelihood, will stay that way.

The most important advice we gave Norma and Jim was to recognize their mother's limitations and lower their expectations. She is so absorbed in caring for her own needs that there is nothing left over to nurture others. If you recognize something of Kate in your own mother, then you can anticipate her reactions and take better control when she visits. For instance, don't give her jobs to do. Don't expect her to help out. Arrange for her to be entertained by your friends or relatives. Then should she offer to do something nice like take you out to dinner, you will be pleasantly surprised. But the secret is not to expect it.

◆

If your parent has always been self-centered, chances are she will remain this way.

If your parent is limited as a caregiver, don't put her in positions that require nurturing.

Her own needs are so great, she has no capacity for understanding the needs of others.

It is natural to think of a self-centered person such as Kate as *selfish*. But to use the word "selfish" is to imply that she has some control over her behavior. She is self-centered because her own needs are so great that she is unable to respond to anyone else's needs. She spends so much emotional energy in keeping herself free from depression that there is very little of herself left to give to others. You may feel sad to let go of the hope that your mother will one day be the nurturing mother you always wanted. But when you do you will be able to feel more peace within yourself about your mother's limited capacity rather than feel she can change if she wants to or if you try something different.

Self-Centeredness and Old Age

As these stories have illustrated, the problems of self-centered people usually become more acute with age. Once preoccupied with building successful careers and families, they now have lost meaningful roles and status in life. Many of the people they surrounded themselves with to give them attention are no longer there—some have died, some have moved, and some have been turned off. Their self-focused world is now punctured by the illnesses and other losses that go with aging, which aggravates their underlying feelings of worthlessness. Their rigid makeup does not allow for much adaptability to the aging process.

The narcissistic people earlier in the chapter are experiencing the expected diminution of powers that eventually comes to all of us. They are repelled by old age and all it implies. Marge's mother can't bear looking old or using a cane or walker, symbols of her aging. Who will adulate her if she is not young and beautiful? Who will make her feel special? Amy's mother is frightened of the implications of her heart disease, not only by the feelings of mortality that everyone experiences but also because she fears her declining health will diminish the approval of those around her. Her desire to move in with her daughter is not simply to obtain help in the face of diminishing physical strength but is also to decrease the chance that her daughter will reject her, along with her need for constant bolstering. Our advice to Amy was guided by the understanding of her mother's expected devastation if she feels she is being rejected.

Self-centered people such as these mothers often develop illnesses as an unconscious way of dealing with their devastating feelings of rejection and of warding off the accompanying depression. It is as though the bad feelings are sloughed off and then attach themselves to a body part and the problem becomes a tangible physical problem, more acceptable than the inner emotional conflict. Often the illness is symbolic of this inner conflict. An example is a woman who suffers from "head hammering" and talks about her clash of feelings in regard to an impending move. A gentleman with gastrointestinal symptoms speaks about swallowing his anger and disappointment. A client with lung disease says his rage toward his irresponsible brother chokes him.

◆

Your parent may develop illnesses (somatize) as a way of dealing with inner conflicts.

These illnesses are real, not imaginary. Be patient.

A geriatric psychiatrist can help your parent with her emotional symptoms.

Your parent may have some hang-ups about psychiatrists. Be careful how you introduce the subject.

Such a person gets very hurt when a doctor treats him hurriedly or impatiently. It is easy for doctors or for you to think your parent's illness is imaginary, but this is not so. The illness is real and it occurs as an automatic reaction at a time of stress, often at a time of separation, such as when you go away on vacation. Grownchildren understandably become very frustrated and even infuriated by such attention-getting behavior. It will help you to relax your anger toward your parent if you understand that this as an unconscious expression of your parent's lifelong struggle against depression and is beyond her control.

Antidepressant medication may be helpful, and it is a good idea to consult an experienced geriatric psychiatrist. You may think this is an easy suggestion to make, but how are you

going to get your parent to agree to see a psychiatrist? One
approach to use with those parents who look to pills as a
magic solution is to introduce to them the doctor as a medication specialist who can help them feel better with their sleeping or whatever symptom they are complaining about. Another
approach is to steer clear of suggesting the doctor on the basis
of psychiatric symptoms, because this may be threatening to
your parent. Instead, you can tell your parent that this doctor
can give her something to relieve her particular physical
complaints.

You Don't Have to Run Away or Give In

It is painful to watch the reaction of self-centered people to
the aging process, particularly when they are your parents.
You may have felt the intensity of your parent's needs while
you were growing up, his anger and devastation if you did not
live up to his expectations, and your own inability to satisfy
him adequately. You learned to be ultrasensitive to his hyper-
sensitivity and often, out of self-protection, to be protective of
his self-esteem.

Here are ways in which some grownchildren of all ages
describe how they feel being with their parent for any length
of time or just by having been raised by a very narcissistic
parent.

- drained after a visit or even a phone contact
- protective of my privacy and my own space
- more sensitive to the needs of others; less sensitive to
  my own feelings and needs
- humiliated about my parent's behavior
- anxious when I am the center of attention, because with
  my parent I never was
- guilty for succeeding
- more secure with facts than feelings; unable to identify
  my own feelings

You may even have become so burdened in catering to

your parent that you left home as soon as you were able. Now you find yourself obligated to come back to help your parent in old age. It is the familiar old burden, only more so now that your parent needs more attention and adulation than ever before and expects it all from you. You may seem to be on a figurative merry-go-round, going around and around trying to boost your parent, to admire him, and do for him, until you get tired or sick or even burned out.

Clearly, giving in to your parent's insatiable appetite for attention and adulation is not good for you. Nor is running away: It's not fair to your parent or yourself. There is a middle way. One thing that often helps is to talk things over with others. Think out loud and listen to how your spouse, or friend, or counselor reacts.

Here is how one woman put it to her friend.

◆

You don't have to run away from your self-centered parent.

You don't have to give in to her insatiable needs.

THERE IS A MIDDLE WAY.

◆

I figured out that if I differ from my mother or don't do what she asks of me, she will feel I'm a horrible daughter. I need to do exactly what she wants or feel exactly like she does to make her happy. Only she doesn't stay happy, and it all falls on me to be the instrument of her happiness. I've decided that it's my responsibility as a daughter to do what I can for her, but I'm not going to sacrifice myself any longer. She won't be as happy, but I can't change that.

◆

Can you feel the weight being lifted off this daughter? She did it herself with concerted thought and working through of her emotions, after years of being on the merry-go-round. She finally realized she cannot make her mother happy.

In another instance, a daughter complained that her mother always ruined family gatherings by intruding on conversations or sulking in a corner or seeking attention in other ways. Instead of the extremes of grinning and bearing the misery on the one hand or of not inviting her mother to future family parties, on the other hand, she sought out a middle way. At the next party, her mother would have manuscripts of her life typed and rolled in a scroll-like fashion. The document would contain a history of the family with a focus on different phases of her interesting life. She would hold court with family members, one by one, to give them this gift and review parts of it with each person. Mother would get her need for attention satisfied without ruining the party. And the preparation of this life review was also fun for this daughter and her mother. It gave them something constructive to do weeks before the party.

◆

Be creative.

Find constructive ways to satisfy your parent's need for attention.

In another example, a son was forever irritated at his mother for always wanting the "top people" to cater to her: the "top lawyer" or the "top doctor." If a "top doctor" referred her to his colleague, for instance, she would be insulted. Once he understood his mother's personality, he stopped fighting her quest for the "best." Instead, he helped her get top treatment.

There is, indeed, a middle way.

5
THE CONTROLLING PERSONALITY

CONTROLLING BEHAVIORS

When your parent:

◆ manipulates others by the use of techniques such as guilt and flattery.

◆ is passive-aggressive, i.e., antagonizes others by behaving passively, e.g., by procrastinating or withdrawing or by other means.

◆ elicits feelings in others that reflect his or her own feelings, such as helplessness or rage.

◆ cannot tolerate differences in things pertaining to lifestyle, ranging from the mundane (eating, dressing) to important values (rearing children).

◆ becomes angry and hostile when the persons they are trying to control don't behave as desired, i.e., don't "heel."

◆ makes demands so excessive that the opposite effect is achieved.

"My mother is a control freak."

These are among the most common words we hear from our clients. Chances are you have said them in exasperation if your parent behaves like the parents in the examples in the previous chapters. Remember the dependent mothers in Chapter 1 who got sick or became hostile to make their children do their bidding. Or the self-centered parents in Chapter 4 who would do anything to force their children to behave in ways that bolstered their images of themselves. These parents cannot help themselves. Their need to control or manipulate others is not conscious. Deep down they are afraid they will not get attended to, that they will be left alone, helpless and unable to fend for themselves. Most of the time there was some early life trauma or difficulty in separating from their mothers that made this basic fear a reality for them. It becomes their lifelong tape. So their life focus is on trying to make sure the *feared abandonment* won't be repeated, and they do this by trying to bind their children to themselves. Suppose a grownchild acts independently of the parent's direction. To the parent, the child has broken the bind—separated—and then she feels alone and abandoned. No wonder she tries to keep this from happening and becomes a control freak.

◆

Understanding these basics will free you to make changes:

• No matter how miserable your parent's controlling ways may make you feel, remember that she feels worse than you do.

• She is suffering from early life experiences that get stirred up in the present.

• Controlling those on whom she depends is one of her most powerful ways of defending against this depression.

Grownchildren have lived with these parental behaviors all their lives, and, as we have seen from the earlier examples, they react in various ways. Often they take the easy way out and remove themselves from their parent's orbit as soon as they can, only to be forced to return later when the parent is older and needs their help. When this happens, not only does the issue of parent care have to be faced, but also the animosities built up over the years of separation have to be overcome. There are also times when a grownchild who attempts to loosen the bonds rather than separate completely is rebuffed by a parent who cannot tolerate anything but complete control. The next story illustrates this.

A CONTROLLING MOTHER WHO CUT OFF HER DAUGHTER NOW NEEDS HER HELP

Susan was a middle-aged woman who came to our office in a crisis situation with a problem that had developed over the years as a result of her mother's need for control. Here are Susan's words.

◆

My sister Betsy called me from California last week. She was frantic. "I can't cope with Mother and Dad anymore. You have got to help me."

My sister took me aback, not because of what she had to say, but because she said it at all. You see, my sister and I had not spoken for twenty years. I have also not spoken to my mother or father for twenty years.

When Stan and I were first married, we lived close to Mom and Dad. Mom used to come over to the house all the time on the spur of the moment, oblivious to whether I was in the middle of something. After a couple of years we moved to another town about twenty miles away. The visits were much less frequent, but not the telephone calls. Mother insisted that I call her every day, first thing in the morning. If she did not receive my call by nine o'clock, I had a lot of explaining to do.

This telephone tether was just one of the many ways my mother tried to keep me tied to her, and it began to drive me crazy. I went to a counselor, who over time gave me the emotional support I needed to loosen the unhealthy connection between us.

I began by telling Mother about my seeing a counselor and that it was important for me to learn to be a little more independent. So when I told Mother that I would be calling a little less frequently, three times a week instead of every day, she really hit the ceiling. I remember these words of hers because they were the last she ever spoke to me: "If it's a three-times-a-week mother that you want, it's a no-times-a-week mother you'll get."

Not only did she cut me out of her life, but she made Dad cut me off, too, and also my sister Betsy. That's why I was so shocked when Betsy called me out of the blue.

Shortly after that incident, I tried to patch things up, but Mother would have none of it. It had to be on her terms or on no terms at all. My many attempts at reconciliation over the years were all rejected. Mother's Day flowers were returned. My sister refused to see me on a trip I made to California when I wrote and phoned, and even when I got Dad alone on the phone once, he said, "You know your mother; it's better not to call. She'll just get mad at me, and I'll be in the doghouse, too."

Mother and Dad moved to Florida a few years ago, and then their health began to deteriorate. Dad showed signs of Alzheimer's, and Mother, some heart problems. I remember that even years ago, Mother used to treat Dad like dirt, but he would pass it off. He loved her so much, he would do anything she wanted, even join her in cutting me off. No matter how nasty she would be to him, he would just shrug his shoulders. Now the situation has gotten so bad, according to Betsy, that she can't stand it anymore. She talks to them every day from California and has gotten to feel so stressed and helpless at a distance that she finally broke down and called me. She said it was my turn to take over. Of course she blamed me for keeping away and not helping out financially all these years.

I felt terrible about being held outside the family for so many years. My children and grandchildren don't know their cousins and other relatives. Betsy is really very much like Mother. They have a tight leash between them that seems to have tightened over the years. I feel bitter toward Betsy for allowing this to happen. But therapy is helping me to appreciate that she may not have the emotional strength that I have to grow up and lead an independent life.

Now I am faced with the problem of getting back into the loop after so many years. I am a long distance away from them, not three thousand miles like Betsy, but still a long distance. Should I hop a plane and run down to Florida?

Would Mother even speak to me? If she does, will she glom on to me like in earlier years? How do I put aside my feelings of hurt and rejection so that I can even face my parents?

◆

Helping the Daughter Decide What to Do and How to Do It

As Susan went on, she became more and more tearful. The years of pain had taken their toll. It seemed to her that she was in a no-win situation. If she made no effort to step in now that she was needed, she could never forgive herself for shirking her responsibility. But if she did step in, she risked the same rejection that had pained her for so many years.

One thing in her favor was the counseling she'd had many years earlier when she was plagued with guilt every time she tried to do something on her own without her mother's involvement. The counselor helped her understand the normal needs for attachment and separation. She came to realize that, painful as it might be, it was important for her own emotional growth and for her marriage that she become more of her own separate person.

Most important, the therapist explained to Susan that her parents were not "bad" people. Rather, they were probably simply victims of their own limitations.

◆

It helps to know that parents like Susan's are victims of their own limitations.

Susan's earlier therapy had helped her live a more satisfying work and family life than she otherwise might have had. This therapy also put her in a position to benefit from further counseling directed at helping her reconnect with her family. The more we discussed the situation, the more Susan recognized she could not ignore her sister's plea. She would have to do something.

But she would not be effective if she acted alone. Everything had to be done together with her sister as a family team to guard against allowing their mother to pit them against each other as she had done in the past. The therapist arranged a conference call between herself and the two sisters to work out the strategy. Once the ground rules were agreed upon, then Susan would step in and give her sister some immediate respite.

♦

Don't let your controlling parent pit you against your siblings.

Whenever possible, take action in concert with other close relatives.

♦

Role-playing is a good way to prepare for difficult confrontations.

Since Susan had been disconnected for so many years, Betsy would take the first step to prepare their mother for Susan's contact. She could do this by phone or in a letter explaining that she called on Susan to help out with the new developments with their dad. Then Susan could follow this up with a phone call or letter telling her mother her plan to come down and get some help arranged.

Betsy followed through as planned, and their mother did not display any overt hostility to the idea of reconnecting with Susan. Yet Susan was still wary. How could she do this without encountering the same old rejection? We advised her it would not be constructive to bring up the twenty-year cutoff, but that her mother might bring it up. Then we did some role-playing to prepare her to handle her mother's negativism or attacks on her without becoming defensive. After several practice sessions, Susan was ready to make the first phone call. This is how it went.

SUSAN: Mom, I know it's been a long time.

MOTHER: Yes, it certainly has. What's on your mind? [*an edge of hostility in her voice.*]

SUSAN: Betsy says Dad isn't well and maybe I could help out a bit.

MOTHER: So Betsy is fed up with me! She needs a fresh replacement, is that it? [*shows a fear that Betsy is leaving the fold*]

SUSAN: Betsy wants my support, and we both want to be here for you. I know Dad is having memory problems and your heart isn't as strong as it was. This must be hard on you, and we want to go through this with you.

MOTHER: Well, don't tell your sister, but she hasn't been keeping up her end of the phone calls lately. We might as well not have a family. [*pits daughters against each other and using guilt as means of control*]

SUSAN: I just finished talking to Betsy. You are right. She hasn't been as attentive because she is exhausted and upset about you and Dad. She needs my support. I need hers. And together, we can be there for you and Dad. How about if I give you a call next week? [*presents a unified and supportive front to her mother and does not react to her guilt-provoking statements*]

MOTHER: I'll be here. I'm not going anywhere.

The next week comes, and Susan phones her mother again.

SUSAN: Hi, Mom.

MOTHER: Susan, I still can't figure out why after all these years you are calling. We've been sick before and you didn't call. I had been resigned to never hearing from you again. And now out of the blue . . . [*feels her daughter cut her off rather than the other way around*]

SUSAN: There have been so many hurts between us over such a long period of time. I want to put all that behind us. I want to make peace with you. Do you think it's possible? [*rehashing who did what to whom would not have been productive*]

MOTHER: We'll see about that.

SUSAN: How's Dad doing?

MOTHER: He's impossible. He gets into everything and then hides things. I tell him to stop, but he likes to drive me crazy. I might have to put him in a home. [*interprets her husband's confused behavior as not obeying her*]

SUSAN: I can imagine how hard this must be. I have a week off from work next month. Why don't I come down and be with you for a few days? [*It would be tempting here*

to educate Mother on the fact that Dad isn't willfully disobeying her, but again, advice is not prudent here.]
MOTHER: It's up to you.

Reentry into the family was the hardest thing Susan ever had to do. The slogan she kept as her mantra throughout this ordeal was: *I'm all grown up. I can choose to feel in control, not controlled.* Susan was no longer blown away by her mother's controlling nature. She expected her mother to be that way and learned how to cope with her the way she was. In fact, Susan was even able to make some plans with her mother that would benefit the entire family.

She began to talk to her mother about getting some relief. Her mother admitted she missed her bridge club and agreed to get out twice a week. Susan was able to bring in a local care manager to meet with both parents in their home and coordinate the help that would be needed for her dad when her mother went out. Susan was careful to introduce the care manager as someone who would help the whole family with these kinds of arrangements as well as with planning next steps and being on call as needed. The goal was to shift some of the parents' dependence to outside helpers. Not only is this a practical way of handling the distance, but it can relieve the stress and worry from both long-distance daughters.

The Queen of the Nursing Home

Susan's mother used control much like the dependent mothers in Chapter 1 as a way of bolstering her feelings of inadequacy. The next vignette demonstrates how a narcissistic person uses control to sustain her inflated sense of herself. The story is told by Jim, whose mother has recently entered a nursing home.

◆

This morning I received a call from my mother's nursing home: "Your mother has been here for three months now, and she is just not getting along with Mrs. Smith, her room-

mate. It has gotten to the point where Mrs. Smith's daughter is insisting that your mother be moved to another room." At the same time, the nursing home administrator let me know that my mother was being a nuisance not only to her room- mate but to the nursing staff as well.

The next day I went over to the nursing home to get more details about the problem. It seems that my mother and Mrs. Smith are attached to each other in a love/hate relationship. They are constantly scrapping, yet they do favors for each other and stand up for each other's rights with the nursing home staff. The problem seems to be that everything is great as long as Mrs. Smith does whatever my mother wants. Then my mother stands up for her, even to the point of calling the nursing home director and the chairman of the board. But if my mother doesn't get everything she wants, there is hell to pay. The incident that led to the phone call was an argu- ment over how wide the window should be open at night. It almost got to the point of violence.

I was afraid something like this would happen. My mother has always considered herself the center of the uni- verse. My dad waited on her hand and foot. He idolized her and called her his queen until his dying day. My sisters went along with her, too, out of self-preservation. I was the only one who objected and so I was usually in her doghouse.

Now my mother says she expects me to take her side and straighten out her roommate. She says if Mrs. Smith is so unhappy that she has to complain to her daughter, then she should be the one to move out.

So you see she is still playing the queen. Only she is now in a different country, where they don't recognize her as royalty. And I'm about to be in the royal doghouse unless I find a way to settle this problem according to my mother's wishes.

◆

What to Do about the Nursing Home Queen

This example shows that when a parent lives in a nursing or retirement home, her behavior is likely to affect her relationship with her fellow residents and the staff of the home as well as her family. This means that any remedies have to involve the staff.

◆

Some ways to give a self-centered parent recognition and mitigate her need for control:

• Make a "This Is Your Life" poster.

• Find special jobs.

• Include her in care conferences.

The advice we gave the son reflected this: We told him that since his mother has acted like a queen all her life, she is not going to change at this stage of life, and so it's foolish to fight it. Instead, we pointed out a number of steps he could take in cooperation with the nursing home staff that would stroke her in constructive ways.

One tangible thing he might do is make a "This Is Your Life" poster with photos and stories featuring his mother and place it on her door or some prominent location acceptable to the home for everyone to admire. This will help her feel better about herself as the nursing home staff becomes acquainted with her life over the earlier span of years when she felt productive. At the same time it will bring plenty of positive attention to boost her self-esteem.

◆

Help your parent find acceptable ways to feel special.

Another approach he might take is to talk to the home about giving his mother a special job, such as placing the flowers on the dining room tables. Since she likes to be first in the dining room, she could be seated first in return for her work. Though it may be impossible to keep his mother boosted all of the time, ideas like this can go a long way in counteracting her need to fight for specialness and control with her roommate and the nursing home staff.

These are constructive ways to boost this mother's ego. There are other things the son can do together with his mother and the nursing home to help in her adjustment. He should

◆

Keep yourself out of control battles between your parent and others.

be able to get the nursing home to include his mother in patient-care conferences. This will help to empower her and will discourage her need to pull in administrators or her son to advocate on her behalf against the staff.

Control over Everyday Behavior

When people have a need to control, they don't distinguish between the important and the less important matters.

One woman complained that her mother was tormenting her twelve-year-old daughter because she didn't conform to her grandmother's standards. Grandma would swoop down on the girl whenever she saw her and smother her with affection. The granddaughter resented this overbearing behavior and pulled away. "She never comes over to kiss me," or, "She is as cold as ice," was the grandmother's complaint to her daughter.

Often, parents are still trying to control the way their grownchildren dress. Here is what one mother said to her forty-year-old daughter: "Do you like wearing clothes that don't fit like that? Do you like looking like that? I would never say that to a stranger. It's because I love you and am concerned how you appear to others."

Then there was the woman who lived a lonely life in a retirement home. Her daughter and son would come to visit her or take her out whenever possible, but other, more distant family members rarely came to visit. One day early in May, her niece, Nancy, decided to pay her a visit. It was an unusually hot day, and Nancy had put on a cool summer dress and was wearing white shoes. Before she could say hello, her aunt was quick to point out that white shoes can only be worn after Memorial Day. Nancy then remembered why her visits were rare.

You might call the mothers in these vignettes critical, and they certainly are. But the purpose of this criticism in each story was the need of the mother to be sure that those around her conformed to her standards of behavior. Why are things that are so trivial to most of us so important to these people? Here are some possible reasons.

The women in the last two examples view their relatives' way of dressing as personal affronts. These controlling people believe that their opinions are facts and that they are right about their views. The granddaughter's choice of clothes is not seen as an expression of the granddaughter's taste, but rather as an act of rejection of her grandmother.

There are other reasons for the controlling behaviors. There are people who don't have enough confidence in themselves to allow a deviation from conventional wisdom. They are afraid they will be criticized if they or those close to them don't follow socially accepted standards of behavior. These are people who feel flat, empty, and deflated, with no confidence in their own opinions. Getting others to agree with and conform to them makes them feel validated, "right," and not so alone. On the other side of the coin, when others don't conform, it brings bad feelings and a sense of being wronged. They learned early in life that "it is bad to be different."

Of course, if you were to agree with and conform to your parent's every taste, then you would be sacrificing your own choices, preferences and, in fact, your identity as a separate person. What appears to be control over trivia such as mode of dress is not trivial at all. It is, in reality, the important issue of maintaining separateness and self-respect. So the $64,000 question is, how do you keep true to the way you dress and to your other individual differences, and get along with your parent at the same time?

Responding to the Control Freak

One way of coping with a control freak is through humor. Here is an example.

MOTHER: Those french fries you are serving don't go with your fancy plates.

DAUGHTER: Oh, you're right. Should I dress up the potato or dress down the plate?

Be careful not to offend with your humorous touch. It can backfire with those who feel that issues of this kind are too serious to be dismissed as a joking matter and who may regard your joke as a personal affront.

Another approach is to respond seriously but with a light touch, as in the next example.

♦

Try humor as a way of responding to the control freak.

MOTHER: You shouldn't wear those white shoes. It's not Memorial Day yet.

DAUGHTER: You're right Mom. How did you ever raise such a nonconformist as me?

Or else try responding with a light touch.

If you let your parent push your buttons by being reactive (i.e., giving in or exploding), then you are giving her the power to control you. In these examples, the daughters were acknowledging their independent ways with a kind of lightness that can work well in many situations.

If your parent doesn't respond well to humor or lightness, then you might try to be direct with gentleness and reassurance. Notice in the following example how the son avoids a rebuttal. Instead, he asserts his separateness while being careful to be respectful of his mother.

♦

Stop the control battle.

Sometimes the best approach is to be direct, but with gentleness and reassurance.

MOTHER: Honey, I know your wife likes the way you comb your hair, but I think it makes you look too old. [*competes with daughter-in-law for influence over son*]

SON: Mom, I know you would like me to comb it your way, and I don't want to make you unhappy, but I like my hair this way. Okay?

MOTHER: Shrugs her shoulder as if to say, who am I to say?

SON: Mom, your opinions are important to me. But I like my hairstyle the way it is. It doesn't have to do with my feelings toward you.

◆

Still another way is to come up with trigger phrases to prevent conflict.

Another way of responding is for you and your parent to come up with a trigger phrase that reminds you both that a control battle is about to happen again. And then hopefully, you can both laugh or at least stop the same old tape from playing. Here are a few phrases grownchildren and their parents have invented that work for them.

I'm me, and you are you.

It's happening again. Let's change the subject.

You and I each have our own special ways.

Different strokes for different folks.

For some families, these phrases are too threatening since they emphasize separation. But for others, these phrases help to nip this kind of interchange in the bud so that the parent or grownchild doesn't end up feeling hurt or angry.

◆

Don't become a control freak yourself and try to make your parent agree with you.

With all these efforts in responding to your controlling parent, it is most important to protect your own position while also respecting your parent's position with sensitivity and kindness. No matter what you do or say, there is no guarantee that your parent will be accepting of your differences. If she doesn't, leave it at that. You don't want to end up a control freak like your parent.

"My Mother Is the World's Greatest Manipulator"

Control can take many forms. Susan's mother was an overt controller. So was Jim's mother. Each of these mothers exercised control in their own particular ways. There are other more subtle ways of exercising control that grownchildren perceive as manipulation. One common way of doing this is to attempt to *buy* control. Clients often tell us stories of parents who take their children and grandchildren out to dinner or buy them expensive gifts and then expect favors in return, angering the children because they feel manipulated. These parents who do this are saying that they are not worthy of attention except as repayment for favors.

There are many other things parents do that make their children and others feel manipulated. For example, when the nursing home queen threatened her roommate to get her way, the roommate felt manipulated. The use of guilt and flattery are other common examples. Another example is when a person lies back passively to get others to do her bidding—sometimes called *passive-aggressive* behavior. All these forms of control are felt to be purposeful manipulation by the grownchild. The parent, however, is driven by insecurities and is not aware of the manipulative implications of her actions. Not only does she deny responsibility, but she is insulted when confronted: "Isn't it natural for a mother to show concern?" "I'm just trying to be helpful." Even when a grownchild believes his mother is the world's greatest manipulator, it can help him a great deal to realize that his mother's controlling behavior is a matter of self-protection.

One client told us how he would call his mother up before going to the grocery store and ask her if she needed anything. Invariably, the reply was, "I am out of everything. Come over and help me make out a shopping list." Or sometimes this same mother would call her son and say meekly, "It's only me. I didn't want to bother you, but I am out of everything again." Taken at face value, these little comments seem harmless enough. But this son knew full well that his mother was quite capable of making out her own shopping list and that she was behaving in this helpless way simply to get his attention. And so he was furious at what he perceived as his mother's at-

◆

Show your parent how to be more self-sufficient.

tempted manipulation. He was relieved when we explained that his mother was not consciously trying to manipulate him, that she felt empty and frightened and that some general reassurance from him was all she needed. He was then able to convince his mother to keep a shopping list herself. "I'll shop for you every week," he said. "In between, we can arrange for the grocery store to deliver to you." The son's altered attitude is helping the mother feel cared for. At the same time it relieves the son of feeling constantly manipulated.

The Martyr

The son in this last example was able to handle his controlling mother relatively simply. It isn't always that easy, especially when the parent plays the role of the martyr. Consider the following example.

◆

"I'll be fine. I don't need any baby-sitter. Go have a good time. You don't need me." Mark's mother spoke those words the day before Thanksgiving. Mark and his wife had been invited to the home of close friends for Thanksgiving dinner. Of course, his mother had been invited, too, but she wasn't sure she wanted to go because she really wanted an invitation to spend the holiday at her daughter's home out of state. When that invitation was not forthcoming, she felt hurt and unloved, and withdrew to spend more hours than ever in her room. Once they realized their mother was not responding to their encouragement to come with them, they said they would try to get a sitter so she wouldn't have to be alone. The above words of martyrdom were her response to the offer.

◆

When the holiday was over, Mark came in for counseling, helpless and powerless about what to do about his mother. He was so angry that it was making him physically sick. She had been living with Mark and his wife, Mary, for two years now. Their youngest child had gone off to college, and the two of them were beginning to savor the freedom of the empty nest. Then along came Mark's mother, who controlled their comings and goings with her fears of being alone. Of course, she wouldn't allow anyone but Mark or Mary to stay with her.

We all know that holiday time can be stressful. Expecting to be invited by certain relatives and weathering the blow of not being invited surely takes its toll, particularly when a parent is hypersensitive to feelings of being left out. Mark's mother felt hurt and expressed it by withdrawing in a passive way that left Mark and Mary feeling angry and manipulated. Only she is not aware of what havoc she is creating in her family. Mark ends up feeling he is being pulled like taffy between his mother and his family.

What a Grownchild Can Do When Faced with a Martyr Parent

Mark and Mary knew their experiment with having Mark's mother live in their home was just not working for any of them. They had two options: Be firm and specify some rules to her to ease the burden on all of them, or face the fact that living together was not working and help his mother find a retirement home nearby. In either case, they could expect hurt feelings. Mark wanted to try the first option. Here is how we advised him to speak to his mother.

◆

The choice of being controlled or being in control is yours.

"Mom, the tension in the house around Thanksgiving made me take a hard look at what is happening between us. I know you didn't want us to leave you alone when we went over to our friends, but you didn't want to come and you didn't want someone else to keep you company here at home. There will be times when Mary and I will be going out for the evening and you will be at home. I want to make a deal with you that we will get a neighbor or a sitter to come stay with you. Let's agree on this."

◆

Assure your parent that you will be there for her, but on terms that are acceptable to you.

Of course, there will be backslides. At these times her son should bring up the agreement that they made as a reminder. The son will also do some backsliding, too. To help him along, he will need to do some emotional work himself or with a counselor on how not to buy in to his mother's controlling ways.

It is helpful for this son or any grownchild to appreciate that a mother's need to control through guilt, passive-aggressiveness, or by buying control stems from a fear of rejection or a fear of feeling worthless. She doesn't consciously think about manipulating. She does what she does to survive. She is really feeling like a helpless and tormented child. Accepting that this is the way she functions psychologically can help this son become less reactive. Instead of feeling that he is a bad person for going out to a holiday dinner without his mother, he can say to himself, "Mom can't help herself. I can't stop her behaviors, but I can stop myself from being controlled and feeling manipulated. I don't have to feel like a bad son—that I have let her down. I will go out as planned and will phone Mother to make sure she is okay." In short, a grownchild does not have to allow himself to be manipulated. He can be in control of himself and his life.

Stress Caused by Controlling Parents

In our experience, of all the difficult behaviors, the controlling behaviors are the ones that seem to cause the most stress in grownchildren. The controllers, especially the subtle ones, are very skilled at hiding their real motives for getting what they want. Indeed, as already pointed out, they don't even know how their behaviors are affecting those close to them. Their indirectness can infuriate others, who may end up feeling like one daughter who said, "My mother is a travel agent giving out guilt trips."

Here are some of the ways in which our clients described

how their controlling and manipulative parents made them feel.

- guilty
- tethered
- confused about mixed messages such as, "Leave me. It's all right," or caring messages such as, "I do this for your own good."
- stymied
- depressed
- guarded about sharing personal thoughts
- rebellious
- powerless

If reactions similar to the above get the better of you, you may want to consider professional help. This may come in the form of a group for caregivers, or individual counseling by a social worker, psychologist, or psychiatrist. The counselor will guide you toward examining your role in your family while you were growing up and your relationship to your siblings and parents. Then she will help you identify your hot buttons and how your parent presses them. It can be extremely beneficial when the counselor helps you understand something about your parent's limitations. Then you will be able to put your parent's and your own behavior in better perspective.

◆

A skilled professional can help you to identify your hot buttons and learn to be less reactive.

In our experience, people who gain insights about themselves and their families are able to find similar patterns with friends and on the job with colleagues and supervisors. The insights you gain from the counseling experience is potentially transferable to life issues beyond your relationship to your parent, and the same skills you develop from these insights in dealing with your parent can be carried over to the workplace.

◆

If your parent lives a
distance away, a care
manager in your
parent's location can
ease the burden on
both of you.

It doesn't matter whether you live close to your parent or thousands of miles away. A parent who feels the need to control will do so wherever she lives, and the stress that it brings the grownchild can be just as great if she lives one thousand miles away as it is if she lives nearby. If your parent lives a distance away, we have found that hiring a care manager in your parent's location can ease some of the burden on both the parent and the grownchildren. She can take care of things locally that your parent is trying to get you to do from a distance, and it sometimes gives a parent a sense of security when there is someone nearby who attends to her needs.

Because it is so important, we will stress the fact that *no matter how miserable your parent's controlling and manipulative ways may make you feel, your parent feels worse than you do.* These controlling behaviors stem from a deep insecurity and a lack of self-esteem that has been a lifelong struggle. Such a parent doesn't feel inwardly worthy of gaining the attention she needs and tries to force it from others in controlling ways. She feels victimized and at the mercy of her impulses and fears. You, her children, and others in her orbit are her rescuers, and she feels tethered to you.

There is no need to continue to be stressed out and even victimized by your controlling parent. It is never too late to get a handle on your own reactions and to change the interaction between you and your parent.

When Reasoning Works

Are there any situations in which you can expect to do more than change the way you deal with your controlling parent? Can you ever expect your parent to back off? The answer is yes, but only in special circumstances.

For example, what if your parent has always tried to control others, but, in contrast to the people earlier in the chapter, has been able to step back and listen to reason? If reasoning has ever worked in the past, then this is the first

◆

You can use reason with a controlling parent when it has worked before.

approach to try. What have you got to lose? If it doesn't work, drop it and try again another time.

It is not always easy for a grownchild to stand up to a controlling parent with kindness and due regard for his feelings. Here is an example of how a daughter was able to respond to her father when he gave unasked for advice on disciplining her child.

DAUGHTER: Dad, when you told me to give Susie a slap on her backside when she wouldn't listen to me, I was more annoyed with you than with my daughter. I just wish you wouldn't tell me what to do. I am perfectly capable of raising Susie. And if I want your advice I will come to you and ask you for it.

DAD: I wasn't telling you what to do. It was just a suggestion.

DAUGHTER: That's not the way I heard it.

That's the way the conversation ended. But Dad mulled over what his daughter said about his butting in and called her back a few days later.

DAD: Honey, I realize that I've been giving unasked for advice. You know I think you are a wonderful mother. I'm just trying to give you the benefit of my years of experience. You've known me long enough to know that tact is not one of my strong points. Your mother reminds me all the time that I always think I'm right. It does get me into trouble.

DAUGHTER: I know, Dad.

DAD: From now on, I am only going to give you suggestions when you ask me. I would love it if you came to me for advice. Sometimes I think I have the answer for you and

I want you to know it. I'm going to really try to keep from butting in on you.

DAUGHTER: That's great, Dad. I may just do that and ask for your opinion sometime. You're not so bad in the advice department.

DAD: [*laughs*]

Notice how the daughter was forthright with her father and respectful at the same time. She didn't focus in on what her father said with a comment like, "Dad, *you* are butting into my business. Back off." Rather, she focused on her own reactions by saying, "*I* was more annoyed with you than with my daughter." This is a tried-and-true communication skill called giving "I messages" instead of "you messages." In this way she was able to show her father how she felt as the result of his attempted control.

This technique can be very effective on the right kind of person. But never try it unless you are sure the controlling person has the ability to look at himself and accept criticism.

◆

Reasoning may also work when the controlling first appears later in life.

Under these circumstances, the controlling may be reversible.

Another situation in which reasoning may work is when the controlling behavior shows up for the first time in later life as a result of some change in the person's life or environment. This is much the same as we described in earlier chapters for other later-life difficult behaviors. Moreover, we saw that not only is it possible to reason with the person about his behavior, but that this behavior is potentially reversible.

Here is an example of a man who tried to control his wife in later-life in response to her worsening Alzheimer's symptoms.

This man's son told us of the situation between his parents when he visited our offices. When his mother's Alzheimer's symptoms became so serious that she could no longer be left alone, his father, a respected federal judge in his late seventies, decided to retire and devote himself to his wife's care. Her doctor explained the nature of the disease and all the behavioral problems he would have to cope with as her memory got progressively worse. Yet when she began to ask the same questions repetitively, hide his papers and books and even his hearing aids, and lose the ability to handle her own dressing and undressing, he would try to reason with her. He would badger her when she did not respond and yell at her when she didn't do as he wished. Their son was getting more and more worried about his dad's impatience with his mother.

Our social work counselor told the son that it was important for us to get a firsthand picture of the interaction between his parents by visiting their home. The son agreed and later that day went to see his father. "Dad," he said, "I can see that Mom is getting worse and that you are stressed. I've called an aging consultant to come tomorrow to check Mom out and give us all some guidance. She will be here at two o'clock." At the counselor's suggestion, his manner of speech was deliberately casual and nonthreatening to avoid resistance from his father, who might well have resented an outsider getting involved in their private family affairs.

When the counselor assessed the situation, she recommended to the father that day care would be helpful for his wife, and she told him about some of the fine senior day-care centers in their area. As devoted as he might be in caring for his wife, the day-care program a couple of days a week would offer her more stimulation than she could get staying home all the time. She also suggested that he might get some practical advice from others in similar situations by joining a support group located at the day-care center. The counselor deliberately did not focus on the relief that he would get from being a caregiver 100 percent of the time. If she did, he might feel guilty that he can't do a good enough job of caring for his wife and is apt to resist her suggestions and hang on even tighter in his current situation to maintain his personal control.

Why should a man who never had a particularly controlling nature become controlling at this time? There are several possible reasons. For one thing, he may feel upset about his life being so out of control and his inability to put order and sense into it. Though he might well deny it, deep down he may resent missing his golden retirement years with his wife. We also have to remember we are dealing with a proud man who has had nothing but success all his life as a lawyer and judge. Why should he not be as successful in caring for his wife as in all his other endeavors? Perhaps it is too painful for him to admit to himself that he is helpless to make his wife better. Trying to force her to behave as he wants her to is the way he reacts.

As controlling as the judge may be, with the right approach he can be reasoned with to examine new approaches that would be helpful to both his wife and himself. If you are facing a similar situation, you should be optimistic that with the proper approach you can persuade your parent to relax his controls.

"I'll Eat as Much as I Want, and Won't Go to a Shrink. He Can't Bring Back My Husband."

6

SELF-ABUSE AND DEPRESSION

SELF-DESTRUCTIVE BEHAVIORS

When your parent:

- has ever been addicted to alcohol, drugs, or medicine.
- has ever had eating disorders, e.g., overeating or refusal to eat.
- has ever behaved compulsively, such as by gambling, hair-pulling, excessive washing, etc.
- has ever been accident-prone.
- behaves masochistically, e.g., doesn't comply with dietary restrictions or refuses to take medication.
- has ever been suicidal or threatened suicide.

No matter how aggravating a grownchild may become with a parent's dependency, turnoffs, self-centeredness, and the like, nothing is as alarming as a parent who behaves in the harmful ways listed above, especially when the self-abuse is potentially suicidal. This is the most worrisome of all the difficult behaviors. We have observed that self-abusive behaviors that start at a young age remain prevalent throughout life. The tendency to suicide remains a grave concern into old age.

What leads a person to take the ultimate step of abusing himself to the point of suicide? The short answer to this question is *depression*. A person can suffer from depression for many

◆

Behaviors such as drinking can mask the underlying depression.

123

reasons. The earlier chapters have described difficult behaviors that are the ways in which some people keep the depression undercover. To this list must be added the self-abusive behaviors that we discuss in this chapter, for example, the use of alcohol or drugs. But these defenses do not work all of the time—sometimes the depression breaks through. When this happens often enough, the sufferers may seek to end their lives in one way or another.

Here is a typical example of a self-abusive older person from our caseload.

A MOTHER WHO HAS TO EAT, SMOKE, DRINK . . .

◆

Anabel had been a resident at one of the nicer retirement homes in her city for three months. She made no effort to adjust to her new surroundings. She refused all opportunities to socialize with her fellow residents; she insisted on having her meals brought to her room instead of going to the beautifully appointed dining room. She refused to participate in any of the activities offered. She spent her days and evenings in front of the television set chain-smoking and eating junk food.

◆

Anabel's daughter, Joan, became alarmed at what seemed to be happening to her mother and came for help. The story she told of her mother's life history was a story of lifelong self-abuse.

◆

Anabel's father was an alcoholic who abused his wife and children. Anabel's first husband, Joan's father, was also an alcoholic. Whenever he got drunk, he beat his wife and often left her for months at a time. Anabel finally had enough of this abuse, divorced her husband and, with the help of her mother, went to work to support herself and her young daughter. However, in this time of her greatest misery, she took up alcohol to help her forget her problems.

A few years later, she married Jack, also an alcoholic. The two of them decided to do something about their addictions, went to Alcoholics Anonymous together, and remained alcohol-free for many years. They were eagerly looking forward to a happy retirement, when Jack died suddenly of a heart attack. Anabel then went to live with her daughter.

It was hard for her to adjust to her new life. She had been very dependent on Jack, and now with him gone she transferred this dependence to Joan. She dropped her friends and activities and had no social life other than that provided by her daughter. She also reverted to her old addictive ways—not to alcohol, but to smoking and eating. In what seemed to Joan like no time at all, Anabel went from a size 6 to 250 pounds. Joan did everything she could think of to snap her mother out of her doldrums. She thought a psychiatrist might be able to prescribe something to curb her mother's appetite. But Anabel refused. "I'll eat as much as I want, and won't go to a shrink. He can't bring back my husband," was her response. It was then that Joan sent her mother to the retirement home in the hope that she could be enticed into a little social activity, get some exercise, and do something other than eat and smoke. When she finally realized that her mother's problems were deeper than a change in environment could cure, Joan came for help.

◆

Helping This Mother Break with the Past—The Use of Letter-writing

Anabel had come from an abusive background and was self-abusive in one way or another from her earliest adult days. Some of the things we pointed out to Joan in exploring her mother's problems were that she had been able to summon up the inner strength to kick the alcohol habit earlier in life and might be able to do it again with her smoking and overeating. For this mother, smoking and eating were the ways she covered her grief over her husband's death, just as earlier in her life she had used alcohol as her crutch. This is how Anabel copes with her world.

Before she came to us, Joan had tried many things to snap her mother out of her self-abusive behaviors. She had talked to her until she was blue in the face. She tried the retirement home approach. She and her younger sister tried confronting their mother together about the way she was damaging her health, but she got angry at them both. They suggested psychotherapy and offered to pay for it, but that only got her angrier. Was there more she could do, Joan asked?

♦

Letter-writing is an effective way to reach your parent and get her to go to counseling.

We suggested another approach that is sometimes successful: letter-writing. Unlike verbal communication, a letter allows one to frame an argument that can sink in over time without being interrupted by an instantaneous negative emotional reaction. This seemed worth trying here, especially since Joan had remembered how at various times in the past they often exchanged letters. If both Joan and her sister wrote letters, their mother would have two important messages to read over and over again in the quiet of her own apartment.

The two sisters worked hard planning out what they wanted to say and met one time together with us to be sure their letters were not attacking and critical. It was important that every message in these letters was genuine and authentic. Here are some of the most important parts of Joan's letter.

This first section tells Anabel how much she means to her daughter. Specific memories of what her mother did for her using "feeling" words are detailed here.

♦

"Mom, I want to express some things I've never said to you before. I think about how you were always there for me when I was young, even when

Dad wasn't. Remember when I had my appendix operation? I was twelve. You didn't hesitate to take two weeks off from work to take care of me. I remember you made a gigantic pot of chicken soup. Every time I awoke from my nap I remember those cooking smells, Mom. I felt so safe and warm with you. I picture the time I came home from high school completely devastated after John broke up with me in the hall after Spanish class. I walked in the door looking forlorn. You immediately got off the phone with your girlfriend and sat down with me. We talked for two hours. You even told me about some of your breakups as a teenager. I'll never forget how loved I felt by you."

◆

The second part of the letter conveys how Joan is affected by her mother's current behavior.

◆

"When I came over last week to join you for the annual Christmas party at your retirement home, I was so taken aback to find you were still in bed. Then I saw that the gift packages of goodies from your friends were strewn all over your bed and that you had gone through a lot of the sweets. This made me so sad. I was so proud of you years ago when you and Jack went to AA together and you were strong enough to kick the habit."

◆

This third section describes the kind of relationship Joan wants to have with her mother in the future. To be effective, she is specific in what she wants from her mother.

◆

"I want to be proud of you again. I want to have my strong mother back. I need your advice about some of the difficulties I'm having with three-year-old Tyler. He's really a handful, and I'd like to start meeting again for lunch on Saturdays so I can talk to you about him and other stuff as well. I want to brag to you about what's happening at work and feel that you're still proud of me. I want us both to feel good about each other again. Mom, I want you back in my life."

◆

In this last section Joan makes a plea for her mother to get professional help.

◆

"Mom, I know it has been awful for you since Jack died, but I know you are strong enough to take it without making a wreck out of yourself, once you make up your mind. I want to feel that I am important enough to you for you to pull your life together for me and your grandchildren. I know it is hard, too hard, in fact, for you to do all by yourself. That's why I have sought out a clinical social worker who I know can give you the kind of help you need to get you through this. Here's her name and phone number. I hope you will decide to go. And, if you do, would you like me to go with you the first time?"

◆

Joan's sister also wrote her mother a letter following the same guidelines. She ended her letter with the same plea for her mother to call the professional that Joan located, listing his name and phone number as well.

Letter-writing can be very effective. Anabel was very moved by her daughters' letters and did go for help. It works with many people, as it did with Anabel. But some situations call for more formal intervention with a professional entering the scene, uninvited by and unknown to the parent until the day of intervention arrives.

A Professional Intervention—A Mother Who Is Drinking Herself to Death

Richard came for help about his alcoholic mother. He began his story with the statement that he could not remember a period of time from his childhood on when she wasn't drinking. Each morning she would take a couple of shots of bourbon, and it was out the door to her job. He would never bring a friend home from school with him for fear that his mother had returned home early and would be sprawled on the couch in a drunken stupor. Yet it is interesting that Richard, like many children of alcoholics, felt he'd had a normal family life. It is also typical that his father could never face up to the problem at all and had always told Richard that he was making a mountain out of a molehill whenever he expressed some concern over his mother's drinking.

Now his mother is seventy-eight years old. Two weeks ago she went into a drunken rage. She ranted and raved, "No one cares about me. All you want is my checkbook." She defecated all over herself. Her husband cleaned her up and put her back to bed loyally and lovingly. "Her life doesn't have to end this way," Richard said. "There must be something we can do for her."

Richard's mother is not the only one with a problem. It is, in reality, a family problem. The mother has had a drinking problem that the father has ignored even when it was disturbing the children. What is different now is that the mother's aging body can no longer tolerate the alcohol levels she could more easily withstand when she was younger and more active. Her reaction to the drinking is now so severe that her children and even her husband are afraid the alcohol is slowly killing her. Something must be done.

A formal *intervention* is called for. This is a structured technique led by an expert in addictions. The technique can be used for people in a medical crisis such as Richard's mother, who will not accept help in more usual ways. For example, it has been used successfully with parents who are not managing by themselves—who are falling, or burning themselves, or overmedicating themselves—and still refuse to make a change in their living arrangements.

◆

When nothing else works, consider a formal "intervention" for a parent in crisis who refuses to take actions for her basic health and safety.

The first step was for the interventionist to meet with Richard, his siblings and their wives, Richard's father, and other significant people in the mother's circle. Some of them—especially the father—were apprehensive and concerned that the intervention process would only make things worse. The interventionist explained to the father that this process of so-called protection had been going on all their married life, and if nothing was done to break this pattern, then the result could be catastrophic. In this way, the interventionist pulled everyone together in an alliance to come up with a well-thought-out plan.

This was done in a series of meetings in which the interventionist went over the mother's life history to heighten the family's sensitivity to and empathy for her plight. The family came to understand that she had been cruelly mistreated as a child and probably abused by her brother (something she never admitted), and never had developed a positive self-image except in her career as a legal secretary. This early mistreatment had left her with a deep depression that she tried to dissolve in alcohol.

The interventionist asked each person to write a script in three parts, similar to the first three sections of Joan's letter to her mother, Anabel. The first part explains how much the mother means to the person; the second part, how the person is affected by the mother's current behavior; and the third part, the kind of relationship that the person would like to have with her.

On the day of intervention, everyone is fully prepared with a script. As you can imagine, it is a very emotional time with the mother confronted by all those most devoted to trying to help her. At the end of the meeting, after everyone has read his script, the interventionist asks the mother to go to a prearranged alcoholic treatment center at that moment. This mother agreed. But what if she hadn't?

The interventionist was aware that this was a real possibility and had worked out a second scenario. The participants would reassemble with another script, this one containing clear statements about what they are prepared to do if the mother continues to resist treatment. Here is a possible statement.

◆

"I love you dearly, but I've come to realize there are certain things I do that make it easier for you to continue drinking. Because I care for you, I cannot in good conscience keep doing these things. If you don't get help, I will no longer speak to you, either in person or on the phone, when I suspect you have been drinking."

◆

◆

SCRIPT

Part 1
How much Mom means to me
•
•
•
•

Part 2
How I am affected by Mom's behavior
•
•
•

Part 3
The kind of relationship I want to have with Mom
•
•
•
•

Selecting an interventionist who fits your family is the key to a successful outcome. He or she should be a trained counselor with experience doing interventions. Above all else, you should feel safe and comfortable with this professional because you are entrusting him to handle a critical matter in your family. Interventionists come from various backgrounds, including social work, drug and alcohol counseling, and clinical psychology. Recently, an Association of Intervention Specialists has been formed. Its address is P.O. Box 3204, Grand Central Station, New York, NY 10163.

"Take My Husband Away or Take Me Away"— Passive Suicide

The protagonists of the foregoing stories were people plagued by depression. They had adopted various self-destructive behaviors during much of their lives to hold down their depression. Such people may become suicidal later in life when the old methods fail. The next story is an example of such a person.

◆

Selma's father died when she was eight years old, and her mother went out to work leaving her with the responsibility of taking care of her two younger brothers. This experience left her scared, helpless, and resentful toward her mother and brothers. But she was also a very intelligent girl who grew up to be an astute businesswoman. At an early age, she married a man without much education and denigrated him all their married life. But he loved her dearly despite her constant criticism, and he persisted in seeking new ways of doing things to please her. Despite the fact that he was beneath her intellectually, something that she let him know almost every day, the marriage stayed together. When both were in their early eighties, he began to show signs of Alzheimer's disease, becoming demented to the point that the couple's children suggested they move into a retirement residence. He was content there, but he was becoming so impaired that he could no longer take her shopping, buy gifts for her, chauffeur her here and there, and take her out to nice restaurants. Now that he could not do these things for her and had become childlike in his dependency on her, the equilibrium of the past was thrown out of kilter: Her negative feelings toward him became stronger, and he no longer could compensate with loving care and attention. Their son recognized the change in his mother and brought her to a psychiatrist who prescribed antidepressant medications. But she refused to take them, and talked about suicide as she screamed out, "Take my no-good husband away from me or take me away from him."

Things got to the point where she was checked into a psychiatric hospital. There in the controlled environment she accepted medications and improved enough to benefit from psychotherapy and be released from the hospital. Of course she denied that the hospital had helped her, but nevertheless she was now able to smile, to sleep, and to be much more patient with her husband.

But the improvement turned out to be temporary. About eight months later, in the face of her husband's increasing dementia, she refused to continue her medication and stopped eating. The depression had won out, and passive suicide was the result.

◆

This story shows the ultimate effect of self-abuse. All her life, Selma had gotten by. Her day-to-day existence was a delicate balance between a productive and satisfying work life and an unhappy home life in which she balanced her distaste for her husband with her dependency on him. But now she was too old to work, and Alzheimer's disease had made her husband into a person who could no longer do things for her as he had done throughout their married life. She felt alone and deserted in her old age.

This dynamic between Selma and her husband is not uncommon in depressed individuals. When the delicate balance shifts, the Selmas of the world are unable to tolerate what they perceive as another loss and abandonment. It is then that the self-destructiveness takes over as it did with Selma.

The Depression Demons

"Depression" has become a common word in our vocabulary. In this book we have been concentrating on people like Selma, who have suffered all their lives with depression based on early traumatic abandonment experiences. When a grownchild observes signs of depression in a parent, he may not know its origin. What he does know is that his parent is miserable and making everyone around him miserable.

When the depression is serious and all-consuming, it is called *clinical depression*. Clinical depression is something that can occur in anyone at any age, whether or not he has been miserable all his life. Its sufferers feel hopeless and sad and, at times, can become severely agitated or withdrawn. They can lose judgment and the ability to reason or think clearly. Their sleeping and eating habits can change dramatically, and they can be disoriented and forgetful.

Clinical depression is often accompanied by *paranoia*—the acceptance of ideas that persist despite facts to the contrary. For example, a sufferer may insist she is being cheated by a helper—"My diamond ring is missing. I'm sure Annie took it." Even a son or daughter is sometimes suspect. One of our clients was a son who came to us because his mother accused him of cheating her. This son regularly handled his mother's finances. She lost her trust in him and began demanding to see all the accounts. Finally she accused him of cheating her. Such distrust is not at all unusual. The most common targets of suspicion and distrust are those upon whom the person is dependent: helpers and grownchildren.

If your mother accuses you, try to reason with her by giving her the facts. When the accusatory tone continues and reasoning no longer works, then it is time to seek professional help. Paranoia is common in older people with sensory losses such as sight and hearing. These people have to use their imagination to fill in the gaps caused by their sensory deficiencies and can more easily lose touch with the realities in their environment. Under these circumstances, the individual may accuse someone else when something goes wrong rather than admit his own loss of control.

Most of the time paranoia has a basis in reality, such as a frail old man living in a dangerous neighborhood who is frightened and distrustful of his neighbors. When he begins to imagine there is a plot in the neighborhood to get him out of his home, then he has become *delusional.*

The symptoms of depression in a parent can often lead their children or other relatives to false ideas of what is wrong. Here is an example in which a son, Arnold, mistook his father's depression for Alzheimer's disease. This is how the son described his father's behavior when he came to see us.

◆

The symptoms of Alzheimer's disease and depression can be similar. Get a professional diagnosis.

◆

Dad had a heart attack last year. It seemed to us that he made a good recovery, and we all expected he would assume his old lifestyle—he used to love to play golf and he led an active social life. After his illness, however, he seemed a different man. Instead of jumping up early in the morning to take in a round of golf, we found him staying in bed until eleven. Try as they might, his former golf buddies never were able to get him back on the links. Of course my brothers and I weren't happy to see these changes, but the thing that has us really upset is his forgetfulness—it is now much worse than it was before the heart attack. He forgets to take his medications and gets confused with his directions when he is driving. But most of all, Dad seems to have lost his will to live. For the first time in his life he is talking about wanting to die. This is not the Dad I used to know. I think he must have Alzheimer's.

◆

This man, in contrast to the earlier examples, never had a destructive nature. He didn't drink or do anything else to excess. These behaviors were appearing for the first time in later life. This son was convinced that his dad had Alzheimer's disease and that he was going to decline progressively over time. The reason he came to us was to obtain help with his father's everyday care.

After hearing his story, we told the son he might be jumping to an unwarranted conclusion about the nature of his father's problem. We suggested that the first order of business was to have his father undergo a thorough medical and psychiatric work-up. When he did this, the doctors concluded that his father had a clinical depression that probably resulted from his heart attack episode. With some antidepressant medication and supportive psychotherapy, the father was a new man, reengaging with life after a relatively short time. His confusion cleared up completely. As is often the situation, this man's depression was producing symptoms that mimicked the characteristics of Alzheimer's Disease or some other dementia. This story had a happy ending because depression is highly treatable and its associated impairments reversible.

♦

Depression may be a symptom of physical illness. Ask your parent's doctor for a differential diagnosis.

But the ending might not have been so happy. The son might have been right the first time. This same set of symptoms as described above—confusion, hopelessness, reclusiveness—might have resulted from any of a number of disabilities, such as a stroke, Alzheimer's disease, diabetes, a brain tumor, Parkinson's disease, lupus, hydrocephalus, hypothyroidism, or heart failure. These same symptoms could also be a reaction to drugs or alcohol. This list of possibilities is not meant to be exhaustive. It is rather to stress the fact that there are not only many ways in which depression can evidence itself but that there are also many possible sources. It is folly for grownchildren to play diagnostician. Only a doctor can make the differential diagnosis that will wend its way through the potential causes, ruling some out and seeking positive evidence for others.

The good news is that whatever else is going on physically with your parent, the depression part is highly treatable. As you can see, your parent's

♦

Depression is highly treatable.

symptoms can present a complex picture. That is for the primary doctor, and possibly a geriatric psychiatrist and neurologist, to diagnose. And in certain instances where the findings are not conclusive, the doctor may suggest a regimen of antidepressants to see if the depression lifts and the confusion goes away.

You can help the physicians with the sorting-out process by providing background information as accurately as possible. One effective way of doing this is to write down a symptoms chronology stating clearly which symptoms are new and which are old. As an example, the son in the last story might have described his father's symptoms in the memo on the next page.

You don't have to be self-destructive or difficult in any other way to get depressed. However, it is not unusual for people who tend to behave in these ways to be depressed one day and be back to their old selves the next. Their children probably have become accustomed to these mood swings. But if the parent fails to pull out of his depression after a few days, that's the time for the grownchild to watch carefully and take some action. Take him to the doctor, or, if he resists, ask his doctor if he will come to the house—even doctors who do not normally make house calls may do so under emergency situations. The doctor will refer you to a psychiatrist (preferably a specialist in geriatrics), and, if your parent won't go, perhaps your doctor will prescribe antidepressant medication himself, after consulting with a geriatric psychiatrist. In extreme cases, you may have to call the police or the Adult Protective Service Agency in your parent's locality (see Chapter 3 for more information about Adult Protective Services).

MEMO

....

To: **Dr. Jones**
From: **Arnold Taylor**
Re: **Richard Taylor**

Symptoms chronology after the heart attack:

June 12, 1996	Hospitalized with heart attack
June 19	Released from hospital
September 1	Health apparently restored
October–November	No effort to resume golf game or attend senior center; started sleeping until 11 or 12 A.M.
November	87-year-old brother died
December	I first noticed that Dad was confusing medications.
February, 1997	Noticed Dad's confusion while driving to grocery store
February	Dad first mentioned desire to stop living

Behavior before the heart attack:

Dad was a social man all his life. He has had no history of depression and has been fairly healthy his whole life. He prided himself on his physical stamina and got vigorous exercise all his life. Since Mom died ten years ago, he joined the senior center and made new friends.

No signs of confusion or despondency.

Finally, the doctor may recommend that your parent be admitted to a psychiatric hospital, or, if your parent has a substance-abuse problem, to a general hospital that has a special substance-abuse program for seniors. Don't buy into your parent's fears about going to a "loony bin." More often than not, these institutions are staffed by highly competent and well-trained people who offer the right kind of psychological attention and care. Hospitalization gets the parent out of her everyday stressful environment into a safe, secure place. It may be the only place in which she can be stabilized with or without medications under controlled conditions.

◆

Don't buy in to your parent's fears about psychiatric hospitals.

They are effective places to get your parent needed help.

Stays in such hospitals are short, usually from one to four weeks. The patient is under the care of a team of professionals headed by a psychiatrist. Make sure that you meet the psychiatrist, and that he is experienced in treating older people. Keep closely connected through the hospital social worker who will be making the discharge plan. Your input to this planning will ensure that your parent will get the services and support needed to keep him from relapsing after discharge.

One option for people after discharge is continued treatment at a psychiatric day treatment center. Such centers, often connected to psychiatric hospitals, offer a structured outpatient program for the patient by a trained staff of specialists. The treatment is usually short-term, and its costs as well as the costs of transportation to the center may be covered by Medicare. These centers can be very effective. For information call the Area Agency on Aging in your parent's locale.

◆

Consider psychiatric day treatment centers for parents who are self-abusive or need stabilization after hospitalization.

You Need Help, Too

If your parent has self-destructive tendencies, you may well benefit from professional help in some form. This might be a single consultation or several sessions with an experienced geriatric social worker or other trained professional. Or it might take the form of short-term counseling or long-term psychotherapy.

This professional will help you come to terms with your parent's problem. That is, she will help you understand the basic reason for your parent's self-destructive tendencies and how the behaviors listed at the beginning of this chapter and other behaviors in the questionnaire at the beginning of the book are the ways your parent has tried to hold his depression down all his life.

This chapter has shown that there are many approaches you can take to help protect your parent from self-destructive tendencies. But sometimes it takes a professional to convince you that there is no magic wand *you* can wave to make the depression go away. Simply understanding this can lift a huge weight off your shoulders.

7

THE PROBLEM OF FEARFULNESS

FEARFULNESS BEHAVIORS

When your parent:

◆ is a worrywart, anxious over real or imagined occurrences.
◆ is subject to panic attacks.
◆ has phobias, such as fear of crowds, germs, etc.
◆ has sleeping problems.
◆ behaves ritualistically and superstitiously.
◆ has magical expectations, e.g., goes doctor shopping to look for a cure.
◆ tends to deny the obvious, e.g., symptoms of illness.
◆ is preoccupied with physical problems, real or imagined.

Fear is one of the most basic human reactions. At some time or another every one of us has experienced some of the fearfulness behaviors in the preceding list. After all, who has not suffered from occasional fits of insomnia? Who has never worried that he or she has some of the symptoms of cancer so publicized in the press? Most of us can deal with fear reasonably well. We bear up under these sources of stress with the loving assistance of family and others. Others have been plagued by extreme anxiety all their lives, and these anxieties have affected not only themselves but those close to them. It is not surprising that people who have been fearful all their lives become even more afraid in their later years. This chapter will explore the reasons for fearfulness in old age and offer suggestions to grownchildren that will help them cope with their parents' fears.

We all know that the later years are filled with almost limitless possibilities for frightening events such as accidents, illnesses, and crime. Diminished vision, hearing impairments, and falling are frightening for elders as they contemplate what these limitations can do to their ability to function independently. As people live longer, their own support networks dwindle with losses of siblings, friends, and even grownchildren. Some people are frightened at the prospect of making any changes in their living arrangements, whether it means bringing helpers into the home or making the more radical change of moving into a retirement home. Such changes are interpreted as the end of independent living.

Another all-pervasive fear is memory loss through Alzheimer's disease or other causes. There is a myth that dementia is inevitable. *This is not true.* Most people do incur a gradual memory slowdown called *age-appropriate memory loss.* This is normal and nondebilitating and not the kind of serious memory difficulty known as dementia that is brought about by brain diseases such as Alzheimer's. Whenever memory loss occurs, the fear of Alzheimer's disease is usually present.

Fear of Alzheimer's disease is only one example of the fear of illness. Don't we all know of older people who had been healthy all their lives and who saw doctors only for annual checkups become suddenly confronted with heart disease, hypertension, breast or prostate cancer? Now they are forced to make regular visits to specialists, change their diets in radical ways, and change their lifestyles to something less stressful. It is natural for anyone who is ill, particularly an older person, to be apprehensive that the illness will get worse and that there will be increased suffering. Then there are those people who are not ill but are afraid they will become ill. In its most extreme form it is called *hypochondria,* the disorder that causes its sufferers to be preoccupied with the details of their bodily functions and the possibility of having disease. Hypochondria is one of the most prevalent mental disorders of older people and is especially common in people who have struggled with personality difficulties all their lives, matching the behaviors in a variety of categories in the difficult behavior questionnaire. We continue with a story about a fearful older woman and her son's struggle in dealing with her.

A Fearful Mother Living at a Distance from Her Son

"My mother and father live two hundred miles away and are not getting by very well. Mother is a handful, and Dad is wearing out. I am worried about both of them and don't know what to do."

These are words that we hear often from grownchildren who are driven to desperation by their inability to cope with the problems of their aging parents. Looking after parents who live somewhere else is difficult under any circumstances. When the parent has a fearful personality, it is all the more difficult.

This particular son, Eric, was spending hour after hour on the phone with his parents and weekend after weekend driving down to their home to give them some firsthand assistance. His mother, Marian, had been hard to live with as long as he could remember, especially because of her fearful nature. But now that she was a lot older, she had become still more fearful. Things had reached the point where she had become more of a burden than his father could readily handle. The two of them needed more help than he could provide from a distance away.

Eric told this story about life with his mother.

◆

Can you imagine anyone being kicked out of kindergarten? Well, that's me. That's because there was a shortage of classroom space that year, and I was absent so much that the teacher thought some other child might make better use of the precious classroom space. And the reason I was absent so much was not that I got sick more often than the other kids, but that my mother was always afraid I would get sick. The least little runny nose was enough to keep me home. The kids would laugh and poke fun when they saw me coming to school wearing a heavy woolen coat and huge galoshes even when there was no sign of rain or snow.

When I got a little older, I realized what she was really concerned about was that she would get sick, not just me. She was always running to doctors about this or that imaginary illness. I also began to realize that getting sick was not her only fear. She always tried her best to avoid crowded places.

Now Mom is seventy-eight years old. She keeps Dad on a short leash. He can only leave the house for a very short time because she is so afraid to be alone. She is also afraid to go outside except for doctor visits. For some time she has had a stomach problem, which a doctor told her was a lactose intolerance. But she refuses to take the pills her doctor gave her. She insists on frequent colonoscopies in case her stomach problems turn into colon cancer.

While she is on the lookout for colon cancer, she thinks she really has a brain tumor. She also imagines she has heart disease. She goes from cardiologist to cardiologist in a vain attempt to find one who will agree with her that something is wrong. It's like a hobby with her.

If all this sounds bizarre, wait until you hear this one. She thinks she has had a stroke. Why? Because she imagines that her facial features have become asymmetrical: one raised eyebrow, wrinkles on only one side of her face, and one sunken-in cheek. "I look like a Picasso," she complains to one and all.

I suppose I could laugh at these things if she were not driving my father up the wall with her preoccupations about her health. She always has nagged and criticized him. Ever since he retired about fifteen years ago, he has done all the shopping and cooking. He is getting older and can't manage as well as he used to. Even in the best of circumstances it would be too much of a chore for him to keep up with all the household responsibilities. But with the stress of my mother continually carping at him for not being more sympathetic to her, and his lack of any freedom, the home situation has become more than he can bear.

I am looking for a way to help my father carry on without increasing the burden on me.

◆

Dealing with the Fearful Parent

Eric was becoming more and more upset as he told his story. He seemed to think that finding some way of introducing help into his parents' home was going to fix all his problems. It was clear that some household help was essential to keep the family on an even keel. We told him we could make arrangements to hire a social worker in his parents' location.

◆

A care manager in your parent's locale can act as your surrogate and arrange for the needed help.

We would brief her on the whole situation, and then she would visit his parents and take responsibility for hiring household help. Her role as Eric's surrogate would be twofold: She would be attending to his parents' needs and would be lifting the day-to-day burdens from his dad's shoulders.

But that was not going to solve all of Eric's problems. No matter how much help was there to make life a bit easier for his father, Eric needed some understanding of what was going on with his mother for his own peace of mind. For one thing, he was carrying with him the emotional baggage of a lifetime. Resentful of his mother's overprotectiveness, he had left home as soon as he was old enough. Now, many years later, when his parents both need help from him, the closer exposure brings back his old resentments and anger, making it all the harder for him to handle an already stressful situation. And the distance between them that was such a relief all these years is now an added burden. It was clear that Eric needed emotional help for himself as much as physical help for his parents.

For Eric to let go of his pent-up aggravation toward his mother, he had to gain some understanding of what impels his mother's fearful behaviors and learn that as bad as he feels, his mother feels worse. In fact, it is easy to imagine the degree of emotional suffering felt by a fearful person such as Marian with her unrelenting fear of serious illness. What did it matter that a battery of doctors had told her she had not suffered from a stroke? Whenever she looked in the mirror she could see all the symptoms regardless of what her husband, her son, and the doctors said.

◆

Dig into your parent's background to understand the basis of her fearful personality.

Marian had been fearful as long as Eric could remember, and long before that, from what he was told. He recalled his mother's story about her mother telling her that she was born a "nervous" baby, and how, as a little child, she had fretted over every little thing. The family nicknamed her "Nervous Nellie" because she would get sick to her stomach every time her mother had to leave the house to do errands. When she was only about five years old her mother was sent away to a TB sanitorium for about a year. Ten years later her mother had to return to the hospital, leaving fifteen-year-old Marian with the responsibility of caring for her younger siblings. All this time her father worked long hours selling dry goods door to door, trying to bring home enough money to feed the family. It may be that Marian as a teenager and then later as an adult was reexperiencing the panic and desertion she must have felt as a five-year-old when her mother was no longer there for her. And even before that we can only imagine how traumatic it must have been for Marian each time her sickly mother became pregnant and was barely able to care for the rest of the family.

Thus, it is not hard to envision Marian as a fearful little baby to start, and then as a fearful little girl who felt neglected. Who could blame her if she worried that she, too, might get TB and have to be sent away? Fears continue to plague her as she ages so that she sees her world as filled with threats to her survival. Her extreme ways of dealing with life are an automatic reaction to these fears. While Eric knew all this, he had never before put it together in a way that explained his mother's overprotectiveness toward him and allowed him to feel some empathy for her at the same time.

Instead of trying to convince her that her fears were groundless and ridiculous, Eric began to empathize with his mother's inner torment and found new energy to help her solve problems. First and foremost, he can now help her accept the whole notion of a care manager. However, just because he decides that this professional could be of help doesn't mean that Marian will be receptive to the idea. But if he handles her sympathetically, she will be more likely to agree to hire a professional who can do things for them that her son cannot do from two hundred miles away. For one thing, the care manager can arrange for home helpers to do cooking, cleaning, or other household tasks that have become too much for her husband. But it can't be just any home helper. A woman such as Marian needs a loving presence with her most of the time who can relieve her husband and son from bearing the full weight of her fearfulness. The care manager can make all their lives a little easier by helping to find a housekeeper with just the right temperament.

◆

You will stop arguing once you understand why your parent is so fearful.

Even when you are able to replace your own anger and frustration with understanding and sympathy, a parent such as Marian remains preoccupied with illness. Don't play doctor the way Eric was doing to determine what is real and what imaginary. The nature and extent of Marian's illnesses are not for him to determine. For both their sakes, he should pull himself out of the role of diagnostician. Sure, she has been to doctor after doctor for each symptom, but she never had a psychiatric evaluation that might lead to some productive treatment for her basic problem of fearfulness. With his mother's permission, he might talk to her doctor about his concerns. It would be helpful to first send the doctor background information on her early life that she might not have told him, especially about her history of fearfulness. It could take the following form.

◆

Don't try to diagnose your parent's problems. That's what doctors are for.

MEMORANDUM

....

To: **Dr. Morse**
From: **Eric Smith**
Subject: **Marian Smith**

The following is some background information about my mother and especially about her fearful nature that may help you with your diagnosis and treatment.

Early Life:
- Nicknamed "Nervous Nellie" because she got sick whenever her mother left the house.
- At age five, she was left with her father when her mother went to a TB sanitorium for a year.
- At age fifteen, her mother returned to the sanitorium, and she was left in charge of her younger siblings.
- Her father was home very little throughout her childhood.

Midlife Fears:
- Extremely afraid that her kids would get sick. Kept them out of school a lot.
- Went from doctor to doctor, even though no medical problems were found.
- Afraid of crowds and elevators.
- Would not drive and leaned on others for all transportation

Later-life Fears
- Afraid to be alone in house. Hates husband to leave.
- Afraid to go outside except to see doctor
- Thinks she has brain tumor, heart disease, stroke (you probably know about some of these).
- Continues to run to many doctors to find one who will agree with her.

My Concerns and Ideas:
- My dad is losing his freedom to come and go.
- Mom has never been treated for her fears.
- Mom sleeps very poorly and might be open to medication.

List of Physicians over Last year:
Date: *Physician*   *Purpose of Visit*   *Current Status*

List of Medications:

This kind of information will help the doctor put your parent's presenting symptoms in fuller context and engage her more effectively. His job is to diagnose and treat her physical ailments and help her to accept a referral to a geriatric psychiatrist for a psychiatric evaluation and treatment for her overwhelming fears. The current view is that there is a biophysiological and genetic predisposition to anxiety, and that a two-pronged approach of medication and talking therapy is the most effective treatment. Don't be surprised if the psychiatrist prescribes and oversees a medication regime and prescribes counseling. This collaborative therapy can provide an excellent treatment program.

We emphasize once again that you should always select a psychiatrist experienced with older people. This is especially important when it comes to the use of psychotropic drugs, the effects of which can be very different on

◆

Get an evaluation of your parent from a geriatric psychiatrist for medication reasons.

younger and older patients. It is sometimes a good idea to consult with psychiatrists of different orientations before settling on one. If you do not have much choice in your parent's community, arrange for a geriatric psychiatrist located elsewhere to act as a consultant for your parent's doctor. Information about trained geriatric psychiatrists can be obtained from the American Association for Geriatric Psychiatry, 7910 Woodmont Ave., Bethesda, MD 20814, (301) 654-7850.

The Validation Approach to Hypochondriasis

In the preceding situation, the grownchild, Eric, could begin to solve his problems once he came to the realization that as bad as he felt, his mother was suffering even more than he. One approach that stems from such a realization is called *validation.*

There are many hypochondriacal people like Marion. In middle life and even in their youth they were constantly running to doctors about real and imagined illnesses. It is only natural that such people would be even more hypochondriacal in their later years, given the added health challenges, and it is only natural that their family members would grow increasingly exasperated with them. Here is an example of another hypochondriacal mother, who has complained of back pains for many years. In the dialogue that follows, we show one of many *wrong* ways in which her daughter might react to her. Then we show how a validation approach is more helpful.

MOTHER: The pain in my back is worse today. I don't know what I am going to do.

DAUGHTER: I'm sure it will feel better tomorrow. Try to relax. *[Unknowingly, she is dismissing what her mother is feeling at the moment.]*

MOTHER: It's easy for you to say. I'm in too much pain to relax right now.

DAUGHTER: Dr. Jones said these relaxation pills should be helping. *[Out of helplessness, she wants to come up with a helpful comment.]*

MOTHER: These pills don't work. They put me to sleep, and I wake up with the same pain. He thinks I'm imagining this pain and that it is all in my head. No one understands.

◆

Practice validation role plays for improved communication.

This conversation didn't do anyone any good. The daughter is trying to be helpful, but she is only making things worse. The mother is left feeling alone with her pain, and her daughter feels frustrated and angry that nothing she says can dissuade her mother from her preoccupation with her pain. Look how much better things are when the daughter recognizes the real pain her mother is suffering.

MOTHER: The pain in my back is worse today. I don't know what I am going to do.

DAUGHTER: I don't know how you can stand it. It must be intolerable. *[acknowledging the reality of the pain]*

MOTHER: It is, but somehow I manage. *[Now that her daughter recognizes her discomfort, she no longer feels the need to continue with her complaints.]*

In this second hypothetical conversation the daughter is *validating* her mother's pain instead of humoring her mother or, even worse, arguing with her or calling her crazy after years of listening to complaints that could not be verified by medical science.

Going back to Eric and Marian, here is how the validation process could help him induce her to have a psychiatric evaluation.

MARIAN: I am glad you came into town for my birthday. But I'm ready to call the whole party off. I'm not feeling up to it.

ERIC: That's a shame, Mother. I was hoping you would be feeling a little better. What's the problem?

MARIAN: How can I feel better when I don't get a good night's sleep?

ERIC: Mother, we both know how important it is for you to get enough sleep. I can just imagine you lying in bed unable to sleep and then feeling groggy all day worrying that the next night will be no better. I know there are medications you can take that will quiet your nerves. I'd like to talk to your doctor about referring you to a specialist who can evaluate your sleep problems and prescribe the right kind of medication.

MARIAN: Eric, dear, I've always been such a nervous one. I don't think any medication will help me. But I guess it wouldn't hurt for you to call Dr. Morse and see what he says.

This process of validation will not cure either of these mothers or any person suffering from hypochondria any more than a physician can. But it can make life a lot easier for the parents and their grownchildren. An anxious parent becomes less anxious when she feels her children believe her and understand her. And then the unsuccessful communication that leaves the grownchild distressed and even desperate can be turned around.

A Mother Relives an Early Trauma

We mentioned that abnormal fearfulness is often the result of events that occurred in the person's childhood. In most situations we can only conjecture—as we did with Marian—about the relationship between early events and adult behavior. Sometimes the situation is more clear cut, as in this next situation. Robert was in a pickle and was looking for a way out. His mother lived with him, and her fearfulness was getting to him and his wife. Robert was looking for a graceful way to get his mother to move.

◆

My mother has been a very fearful woman as long as I can remember, especially around water. For instance, when I was about ten years old, I was invited to a friend's birthday party held at a local park. I was the only kid whose mother had to come along. All the other kids went wading in a stream, and when I joined them my mother pulled me out. Was I embarrassed.

My mother has always been afraid of death. She wouldn't allow any talk about dying in her presence. When my father died, she refused to go to the funeral. She never cried or talked about him other than to exclaim, "How could you do this to me, George!"

As she has grown older, she has become more and more controlled by her terrors, worries, and rituals. She's afraid to be left alone. She is so fearful of germs and food contamination that she has become a virtual prisoner in our home, and I feel seduced into the role of guard. Recently we were all invited to the home of friends for Christmas dinner. Mother wasn't sure she wanted to go, because she might be sick. This negative attitude drove me crazy. I would alternately try to be patient and to reason with her and get her to change her attitude. I ended up losing my temper and then feeling guilty and miserable.

This wasn't so bad when our kids were home, but now that they are all off to college, my wife and I are more tied down than ever as she is now afraid to be left alone.

◆

It was then that Robert went into the traumatic events of his mother's childhood and told the story as he learned it from family folklore.

◆

She was born and brought up in a small European town. Her grandmother lived alone in a little cottage out of town. Her mother gave her the job of walking over to Grandma's each afternoon and spending the night with her. There was only one bed in the house, so the two of them slept in the same bed. On one of her daily trips to her grandmother's cottage, she fell into a river and almost drowned. On another night, she woke up in the morning to find her grandmother lying beside her motionless. She had died during the night. All this had happened when the little girl was seven or eight years old, and her terrors have remained with her over her lifetime so that she continues to have terrible nightmares of that childhood event.

◆

Early Trauma Takes Its Toll—Post-Traumatic Stress

In seeking ways of helping Robert with his problems, knowing his mother's early history led us to hypothesize the relationship between her childhood experiences and her later fearful behaviors. Her near drowning as a child explains her fear of water. Her fear of funerals, germs, and other things associated with death undoubtedly stems from her childhood experience with her grandmother's death. Some of her other rituals, such as her cleanliness, fussiness about food, and trying to maintain a fixed daily routine, can be understood as ways of trying to gain some control over her environment in contrast to child-hood events that got out of her control. People with histories and symptoms like Robert's mother are victims of *post-traumatic stress disorder (PTSD)*.

PTSD is the clinical name given to the reactions suffered by a person who has been subject to life-threatening experiences such as physical and sexual violence, war, criminal acts, natural disasters, and sudden loss of people or possessions.

Studies of PTSD have shown that its psychological legacy does not always follow immediately after the stressful events; in fact, many years may elapse before symptoms are noted. Nor does the passage of time necessarily heal the trauma. To the contrary, the fears are often intensified with the aging process and its attendant illnesses and losses of all kinds. Gladys, for example, suffers more anxiety in her later years, seventy years after the childhood events that probably precipitated it all.

Victims reexperience the trauma and its associated fears with reminder events. And so it is only natural that such people try their best to avoid situations that can bring such painful memories. So, for example, Robert's mother avoids situations associated with death—even her husband's funeral—that remind her of the trauma of waking up next to her dead grandmother as a small child. But stressful situations cannot always be avoided. So when Robert joined the other children playing in the stream, his mother experienced an anxiety reaction that led her to yank him out of the water. She was most likely reexperiencing the trauma of her own brush with death as a child.

Helping the Grownchild of a PTSD Sufferer

The first step in helping the grown-child of a difficult parent is to get him to understand his parent's problems and to come to realize the extent of her suffering. Robert came to us looking for a way of getting his mother out of his house and into a retirement resi-

◆

Basic information about PTSD will help make sense of a parent's seemingly senseless behavior.

dence. After some counseling, he learned ways of understanding and then of coping that made such steps unnecessary. Some basic information about PTSD helped him make sense out of his mother's peculiar behavior, for example, why she reacted as she did to his father's death. He now understood that she shut down her emotions for fear of reliving her childhood trauma and for her emotional self-protection.

We found that a role play was very helpful in showing Robert successful and unsuccessful ways of dealing with his mother. For example, we got him to role-play the incident he told us about on his first visit to show him how his own reactions to his mother were not helpful to either one of them. In this reenactment, the counselor played the mother, and Robert played himself.

ROBERT: Mom, we've been invited to the Sauls' down the street for dinner Saturday night. They especially want you to come.

MOTHER: No, I don't go out at night. Give them my apologies.

ROBERT: Please come, Mom, I would really appreciate it.

MOTHER: *[with anger]* Don't bother me. I'm not going, and that's final.

ROBERT: *[with exasperation in his voice]* Mom, you're becoming like a hermit. You never want to be left alone, but you refuse to let us hire anyone to stay with you. Do you expect us to stay home with you again?

MOTHER: Leave me alone. You don't understand. *[she begins to cry.]*

ROBERT: *[leaves the room feeling guilty]*

This role play showed Robert that his reaction to his mother's peculiar behavior was not helping. Robert naturally wanted his mother to go out and enjoy life more, but felt discouraged, defeated, and angry when she refused. If he gave in and stayed home with her, he felt resentful. If he went without her, he felt guilty. He was caught up in a battle between her fears and his own guilt, which left him feeling like a loser every time.

During this dialogue Robert's attitude was governed by his assumption that his mother could be talked out of her peculiar behavior once he convinced her how foolish it was. He was making no connection between the traumatic events of her childhood and her behavior in adulthood. But once we explained something about PTSD and the nature of his mother's underlying problem, he then realized the only way of improving the situation was for him to act differently toward his mother. We made sure this awareness was fortified with a replay of the preceding dialogue.

ROBERT: Mom, we've been invited to the Sauls' down the street for dinner Saturday night. They especially want you to come.

MOTHER: No, I don't go out at night. Give them my apologies.

ROBERT: We'll miss your company, but we are going to go anyway. We'll be back by eleven o'clock. Here's our telephone number. Would you like someone to stay with you and keep you company?

Notice that in this role play Robert didn't argue with his mother or sacrifice himself to stay home with her. Instead, he accepted her refusal and made sure to tell her when he would return. By accepting her decision without an argument, he avoided a confrontation and the feelings that come over the loss of a battle of wills. Rather, he became more sensitive to how his own words and behavior affected his mother, how some of the things that he did or said before were bound to have stirred up her early fears, and what he could do and say, instead, to help her feel more secure.

We were able to get Robert to stop acting out his negative feelings toward his mother. Before, whenever she would bring up her fears of germs at

◆

Understanding helps you control your anger.

dinnertime, he would either scoff at her or tease her, invariably leading to an unpleasant exchange between the two of them. Now that he had some understanding of why she behaved this way, he stopped arguing with her.

As with many grownchildren described in this book, Robert stopped trying so hard to get his parent to act more "normally" once he gained some understanding of his parent's real prob-

◆

Understanding helps you begin to feel sympathy for your parent.

lem. Robert's anger began to turn to sympathy as he became aware of his mother's traumatic early experiences and the effect on her in later life.

Robert began to feel sad and sorry for his mother. He thought about all her suffering in her early years. Instead of getting angry with his mother, he became angry at the circumstances in her childhood that thrust such adult responsibilities on such a little girl. He began to imag-

◆

Understanding helps you to let go of unrealistic hopes.

ine how different her life would have been if these events had not happened. He also tried to imagine how different his own life might have been if his mother had been a different kind of person. Robert finally realized that try as he might, he would never have the kind of mother he had hoped for.

It was a great relief for Robert to realize that his mother was being controlled by her history rather than by her interactions with him. He became more sensitive to how his own words and behaviors affected his mother, how some of the things he did or said before were bound to have stirred up his mother's early fears, and what he could do and say, instead, to help his mother feel more secure. For example, he now made sure his mother knew where he was and when he would return.

◆

A support group can be very effective with guilt.

After the success of a few counseling sessions, we urged Robert to reinforce his newfound understanding by joining a support group. Once a month he met with a group of grownchildren like himself under the guidance of a facilitator. An especially helpful activity in the group for Robert was more of the same kind of role-playing described previously. Other group members played the role of his mother. This additional practice helped him put aside his defensiveness and made him feel more at ease in his day-to-day interactions at home. Here is an example of such a role play.

ROBERT: Phyllis and I have been invited to my boss's house for brunch at eleven o'clock next Sunday, so we can't eat with you as usual at that time. Would you like us to leave brunch for you, or have Mabel (a housekeeper) prepare it for you and join you at the table?

MOTHER: *[with irritation]* You had to be invited at the same time as we eat.

ROBERT: Mom, I'm sorry. I know how you look forward to Sunday brunch with us.

MOTHER: Go. What do I care.

The "old" Robert would have been devastated by guilt in this situation. But his sessions with us and the role-playing in the group helped make him much less vulnerable to his mother's guilt-provoking behavior.

Many grownchildren come to us and say, "My mother makes me feel guilty all the time," as if the mother has the problem. We help our clients see that the problem of feeling guilty or not feeling guilty is a choice of the grownchild. In the above role play the support group helped fortify Robert in rejecting the guilt. He was kind to his mother, but also kind to himself.

See if techniques like this work for you. Be realistic. Changing your own set of attitudes isn't easy. It takes a lot of practice. Counseling, either individual or group, can be very helpful, as it was with Robert.

Here is another example of a grownchild stymied by her guilt. Susan, who lived one thousand miles away from her mother, found her annual visits to be so guilt laden that she resolved to get some help. Fortunately she was able to find a group of people with similar problems. After a few months with the group and a lot of role-playing, she was able to make her next visit much less unpleasant. Here is a sample of a recent conversation with her mother that shows how Susan benefited from the group role plays and support.

SUSAN: We'll be staying with you for two days in June.
MOTHER: Oh, so I'm a two-day-stay kind of mother. How many days are you taking off for your vacation?
SUSAN: Mom, let's try to make these two days really special. I'm sorry it doesn't feel like enough time for you.
MOTHER: I'll take the crumbs. I'm used to crumbs.
SUSAN: Oh, Mom. Come on. *[She changes the subject and fills her in on the details of her daughter's birthday party.]*

Susan didn't digest the guilt. She validated her mother's feelings and knew she wasn't a bad daughter.

You will like yourself and your parent better when you learn to live your life the way you choose rather than be controlled by your parent's reaction. As in the earlier role play, Robert planned his own activities while being responsible for seeing that his mother was well cared for. He knew that he could not make her be accepting, but he felt in control of himself for the first time in many years.

◆ Begin acting instead of reacting.

People suffering from PTSD do their best all their lives to repress or keep out of their awareness those early traumatic events that have had such a profound effect on their emotions. Erik Erikson, the great psychoanalytic scholar, has theorized that the major task of the later years is a summing up of one's life experiences—to achieve a positive and loving acceptance of one's life and oneself. He calls this task *integration.* To achieve this integration status, a person has to be able to mourn the losses and traumas of a lifetime. PTSD victims are unable to do this. We have more to say about this in the next chapter.

8

LOSS, GRIEF, AND MOURNING

Old age is a time of summation, a time when each of us tries
to come to terms with the life that we have been living and
that will ultimately end. Especially important is how we have
handled our losses throughout our lives. As Judith Viorst wrote
in her insightful book, *Necessary Losses*, "The people we are
and the lives that we lead are determined, for better or worse,
by our loss experiences." We suffer losses all through our
lives. The older we get, the more these losses multiply. The
losses are of many varieties: the loss of loved ones, the loss of
companionship, privacy, independence, familiar surroundings,
the loss of physical capacity—vision, hearing, general health,
beauty, the ability to drive a car and other forms of mobility—
the loss of mental capacity, especially memory, the loss of
one's life work that comes with retirement, and ultimately, of
course, the loss of one's own life.

Viorst's thesis is that "these losses are necessary because
we grow by losing, leaving, and letting go." How fortunate is
the older person who is able to face up to his losses, mourn
them, and move on again toward what Erik Erikson calls "a
position of dignity." But not all are this fortunate. Some have
spent their lives developing defenses against life's traumas. To
some, mourning means letting one's guard down, remembering
the old demons, and reexperiencing the painful separations of
early life—the inability to cope with the first of Viorst's necessary losses, separation from the mother. To others, mourning
a loss means reopening the wounds of early abuse that are too
painful to confront.

This chapter will guide you in the ways in which you can be of real help to your parents who have special difficulty in facing loss and in grieving those losses.

Facing up to Loss in a Healthy Way

Most people cope with the losses of old age and move on with their lives. They may react to the losses with shock, disbelief, denial, withdrawal from people, fatigue, illness, increased dependency, anxiety, and depression. But with time and the support of others they learn to come to terms with the loss, recover, and eventually adapt to their changed life. One such person is Simon.

◆

Simon and his ailing wife, both eighty-five years old, recently had moved from their hometown into a nursing home in their daughter's city. Simon finally made the hard decision when he realized he could no longer provide the kind of care that his ailing wife needed. As sad as he felt to give up the past, it was more important to be near his family so that he could lean on them as necessary and make it easier for them to help.

As difficult as the move was, Simon's attitude was one of appreciation for what his daughters and the nursing home staff could do for them. He was able to recognize the positive aspects of his new life and put his enormous losses in place. But in just three months Simon was struck with other losses. First his wife of sixty years died, and shortly thereafter he had to undergo surgery that left him wheelchair bound. It seemed almost too much to expect a man of his age mourning for his wife to have the motivation to rehabilitate himself from his surgery.

But Simon was motivated and worked very hard at his therapies. He was able to share his sadness over his wife's death with others and get support. A social worker encouraged him to reminisce and review his life story as a way of putting his life in place, accepting it, and moving forward. She took him out to restaurants, concerts, and lectures. The stimulation of these activities helped him keep his mind alert and maintain a positive attitude toward life.

◆

Simon's optimistic outlook was largely responsible for his recovery from his surgery. But as he grew into his nineties, he began to lose his newly found health piece by piece, each loss imposing further limitations on his activities. Yet through all this he retained the ability to find joy and pleasure in his everyday life. He had a basic sense of trust in others that allowed him to accept help and he was able to maintain his dignity through his physical decline until the end.

The Losses of Old Age

Consider for a moment the long and varied list of losses that Simon suffered in his later years.

his home and the other familiar surroundings of his hometown

his old friends

his independence

his privacy

his wife

his health

his mobility

It is unfortunate that losses in the later years come in bunches. Still, many of us are inclined to emphasize the loss of loved ones and perhaps not even recognize the others as losses that also have to be dealt with. For Simon all the other losses made coping with the loss of his wife that much harder.

Your parent may be dealing with losses similar to Simon's. Sometimes one loss will beget another. For example, when a person loses mobility from a fall or a stroke, he may require a full-time helper. As necessary as the helper may be, it means the person also loses some independence and privacy along with the mobility.

Most people learn to accept their losses as Simon did and find activities that satisfy them within their more limited physical capabilities. Others get stuck in grieving over their lost capabilities and cannot move on. The people who have the worst time with losses in its many forms—and, in turn, are the hardest for their grownchildren to deal with—are those who have been difficult all their lives. Even if your parent is in this latter category, do not despair. When you understand the way your parent's lifelong condition affects his reaction to loss and you modify your behavior toward him, then you can look forward to different reactions on his part.

◆

Remember that difficult parents have an especially difficult time with losses.

Children sometimes can't bear to hear the complaints of their parent suffering from loss and they turn her off. It's a big mistake. Hear her out. For example, if your self-centered mother has always been vain about her personal appearance, be sympathetic and considerate when she laments her loss of beauty. If your dad has lost his hearing and is behaving in a paranoid manner, be patient and find ways of communicating with him. If your critical, negative mother does nothing but complain about the apartment she has just moved into after decades in her own home, recognize that she has suffered a loss that has to be mourned and treat her patiently. If your parent can't adjust to retirement and is acting out in ways that make you want to get away, hang in there. Even if he cuts you off, try to keep the lines of communication open and be ready to get him back into the fold.

It is understandable that the hardest loss to bear, especially for older people with lifelong personality difficulties, is the loss of a spouse. Grownchildren are always coming to us about a difficult parent whose spouse has recently died. Often the parent's reaction is bewildering, and coping with it while mourning the deceased parent at the same time is more than the grownchild can bear. The next several sections give examples of such behavior with tips to the children on how to cope with their parent's behavior and their own feelings as well.

A Woman Who Couldn't Grieve

You may know someone, either a family member or friend or acquaintance, who recently lost a loved one but acts as if nothing had happened. There are no tears, and there is no apparent disruption in their lives. One client, Sid, was bewildered by that fact that three weeks after his dad's death, his mother, Sarah, still hadn't shed a tear. She got rid of her husband's belongings and mementos in a businesslike way. She was eager to leave their home of sixty years and move into a retirement home. Sid had no understanding of why his mother reacted as she did to his father's death. To make matters worse, she became more and more demanding of his attention so that nothing he did was enough. She found fault with his wife and his children, muttering behind their backs about how selfish they were.

Sid told us something of his mother's background. Her father had abandoned the family when she was a child, and her mother had clung to her all through her childhood. Sarah had once confided to her son that she'd married his father to get away from her mother. Sid had always noticed how similar his mother was to his grandmother: They were both very critical people who had to have things their way. All the time he was growing up, his mother would blow hot and cold on both him and his father. He was either very good or terrible, depending on her whims. He finally escaped when he went off to college. Then when he married, his mother gave his wife a terrible time. "Can't she ever do anything right?" she would ask. So Sid kept away from his mother as much as possible, until his father developed the cancer that finally killed him. Then she showed no tears and no reaction that anything important had happened in her life. Sid sensed that she would need some help in adjusting to her new situation, and that was what brought him to our offices.

We assigned one of our social work assistants, Linda, to visit Sarah weekly to provide her with companionship as well as to do practical tasks such as take her to the doctor and to the drugstore. Linda used family photos to get her to reminisce, first about her career as a schoolteacher, then later about her years with her husband.

Sarah could never forgive her husband for dying. To her this was abandonment, just as when her father had left the family when she was a child. A child does not have the emotional skills to grieve, and thus Sarah was stuck with an inability to deal with separation of any kind. Someone without her emotional baggage would have gotten over the shock of the loss, come to terms with it, and gone on with her life. Sarah could not do this on her own.

Gradually, in her relationship with Linda, and through their photo project, Sarah was given a chance to review her life and to balance some of her negative feelings toward her marriage with some of the happier moments.

We helped Sid understand the impact of his mother's early life on her present situation so that he was better able to depersonalize her complaints and no longer feel he was to blame for her unhappiness. Finally Sid was able to accept his mother's shortcomings. This change of attitude showed in his kinder reactions to his mother's complaining.

What to Do When Your Parent Has Trouble Grieving

If your parent reacted to a loss like Sarah did, without the usual signs of grieving, you may even have felt relieved that you didn't have to cope with her uncontrolled carrying on. While it may be a relief in the short term, it will surely not be in the long term. Repressed grief reactions leading to full-blown depression and threats of suicide can surface months or even years later, often on holidays and anniversary dates. Sarah's repressed grief came out as anger, bitterness, and hostility, the way she had always reacted when faced with losses since childhood. In other people it comes out as physical complaints and illnesses.

Here are a few suggestions for what you can do about your parent's masked grief.

◆

If your parent shows no grief, it's because she can't grieve. It's part of her personality difficulty.

Try to understand that your parent cannot grieve. This failure to grieve is an important facet of her life-long problems. People like Sarah have built strong protective coping mechanisms to shield them from life's greatest losses. Recognize that a failure to grieve does not mean your parent had no feelings or only bad feelings for her spouse. Quite the contrary, people such as Sarah do have positive as well as negative feelings. These mixed feelings are what is so troublesome for the Sarahs of this world. They are emotionally unable to meld conflicting feelings toward one individual, so the problem remains ready to fester whenever conditions of loss threaten.

◆

It doesn't work to try to talk her out of her depression.

Listen to what your parent has to say. If your mother tells you she feels depressed, it may mean her grief is coming out as depression. Don't try to talk her out of it, as the daughter did in the following dialogue.

MOTHER: I don't want to face the morning.

DAUGHTER: *[tries to talk her out of it]* But you have a good life. You have a lovely home. You have two beautiful grandchildren.

MOTHER: Yes, I know, but your father left me alone. I'm all alone here. And I don't feel well.

DAUGHTER: *[Desperate to make her mother happier, she tries to have her mother look at life more optimistically.]* But,

Mom, if you only could see your cup half full, you would be happier.

MOTHER: I'm tired.

This daughter saw how depressed her mother was and tried a dose of optimism to pull her out of it. But it's a lose-lose situation. The daughter got nowhere and felt like a failure. And her mother felt tired and misunderstood.

◆

Watch for signs of grief in your parent's comments.

This mother is trying to grieve just a little bit in the only way she can. You can tell that from some of her comments:

"Your father left me alone."

"I'm all alone here."

"I'm tired."

At first glance, these comments reflect only anger and bitterness. But when you consider how this mother has behaved all her life, you realize

◆

Encourage your parent to air her feelings.

they are the only ways she is capable of expressing her feelings at the loss of her husband. Her grief is masked by physical and emotional complaints and is her way of feeling the loss of her husband. The important thing is that she is airing her feelings, and her daughter will obtain the best results for her mother and herself if she says as little as possible and allows her mother to express her feelings as much as she is able. Here's an example.

MOTHER: I don't want to face the morning.

DAUGHTER: *[says very little]* I know.

MOTHER: Your father left me alone. And I feel sick.

DAUGHTER: *[again says very little]* Uh-huh.

MOTHER: *[beginning to open up more]* I think he wanted to die so he wouldn't have to do things for me anymore. He always hated doing errands like grocery shopping. He hated doing a lot of things for me. I hope he's satisfied. He won't have to come to my aid anymore!

Put yourself in this daughter's position. Here she is sitting by with hardly any response as her mother is bad-mouthing her dead father. It's very tempting for her to jump on her mother at this moment. But it will only make things worse. As hard as it might be, the best thing the daughter can do is validate her mother's negative feelings toward her dad.

MOTHER: He won't have to come to my aid anymore!
DAUGHTER: That's right. And you are left alone.
MOTHER: *[weeping a bit]* Thank God I have you.

By listening and validating your mother's feelings, even the negative ones, it doesn't mean you are agreeing or siding with your mother or being disloyal to your father. It means you have decided that the best way to be with your mother is by not battling her, disagreeing with her, or talking her out of her feelings.

◆

Reminisce about years past. Put together an oral history or scrapbook with photos.

Sometimes reminiscing will help your parent grieve. A helpful technique is to pull out some old photograph albums and help your parent talk about the old days both good and bad, about the days of courtship and marriage, and other special family events. While you can both chuckle together about the funny clothes and bathing suits that people wore in those good old days, the main purpose of this activity is to help your parent moderate negative and positive feelings. For example, if your mother has suddenly placed her deceased sister on a pedestal and can only talk about how wonderful she was, you can gently remind her how difficult Aunt Eva could be at times.

◆

Bring in another person to give your parent added attention.

If such activities don't work immediately after the loss, try them again at a later time. If doing this is too difficult for you, perhaps someone else can do it more objectively. Remember how

Sarah's social work assistant was able to get Sarah to reminisce in a constructive way by helping her recollect the pleasant experiences of her life? Projects such as putting together a "This Is Your Life" scrapbook or assisting the person to tape-record an oral history are good ways to get people to review their past life achievements.

Empower your parent by encouraging involvement and independence. People who are unable to grieve often withdraw into their shells and cling to

◆

Encourage involvement and independence.

a grownchild or other caregiver, expecting to be cared for and wanting all decisions to be made for them. Sarah behaved in this way. In such instances, it is important the person be empowered to take part in the world as much as possible, especially to make their own decisions to whatever extent they can. To ease the burden when decisions have to be made, it is most helpful for a grownchild to predigest the options and reduce the number of alternatives to two or three.

At the same time as you are being sympathetic to your parent, be sympathetic to yourself. For example, if your parent's reaction at a time of loss is to cling to you or make excessive demands, decide what you can reasonably do and what is too much. Setting limits in this way will be best for both of you in the

◆

Be sure to take care of yourself.

Don't let your parent split you from your siblings.

long run. Your parent in grief may also do things that pit you against your siblings. If you understand she has trouble relating positively to more than one child at a time, you and your siblings can arrange individual visits with her and prevent her from causing family rifts.

What to Do When Your Parent Can't Stop Grieving

While people like Sarah cannot shed a tear over their loved ones, there are others who are nonstop grievers. The perpetual griever seems to be as unlike Sarah as can be. Yet, in reality, she is very similar, because, like Sarah, she does not have the capacity to mourn in a healthy way. Understandably, grownchildren of such parents feel quite desperate when, seemingly, no matter what they do, they are forced to watch their parents stay frozen in grief.

◆

If your parent can't stop crying, don't walk out on her or cut her off. That can make things worse.

There are some simple steps you can take that will help your parent get on with her life. First: Gain some understanding of the basis of your parent's uncontrollable grief. Second: Act toward her in ways that neither shut off nor add fuel to her grief. Third: Involve your parent in meaningful projects and activities.

Here is one daughter's story, followed by specific tips based on these three steps.

◆

If the tears wear out both of you, come prepared with a project or activity when you visit.

◆

My father has been dead for twenty years, and it's as if it were yesterday for Mom. At this moment, I'm sure she's on the phone with her sister crying over Pop, saying "What's it all for?" I used to walk out on her when she started in. I felt like a cold, unfeeling person doing that, but I couldn't stand her tears after five, ten, fifteen years. And no matter what I said, she wouldn't stop wailing.

With some outside help, I learned why she acts this way and it has helped me control my own frustration. She still cries a lot, but I don't walk out on her anymore. I no longer take it personally. I now realize Mom was angry with Pop for leaving her and that this was based on painful feelings from her childhood when she was indeed left by her sick parents to the care of an aunt. This understanding has made a big difference in my attitude toward my mother. For one thing, I no longer think I am the cause of my mother's unhappiness. I am more patient and considerate these days.

◆

◆

The counselor taught me how to visit with Mom in ways that work better for both of us. Now I usually come prepared with a project or activity. Here is a list of things we have done over the last year. I think they have been good for both of us.

- *We put together a family album with stories and photos we collected from relatives spread out over the world.*
- *One weekend I took her to my office to show her what I do at work.*
- *We visited friends of hers and mine.*
- *We went to movies and plays. I made sure to pick upbeat ones.*
- *I started collecting teacups with Mom, and we went on antique outings together.*
- *We took a sight-seeing bus tour of the city.*

I now find my visits with Mom are a challenge rather than a dreaded chore. I don't get triggered by her crying as I used to. Instead, I am able to feel sympathetic.

◆

Some Parents Avoid Grief by Replacing

We have seen two seemingly polar ways in which people who cannot mourn express their feelings. Another common way of avoiding the mourning process is by replacing the lost spouse with someone else. You may know of a person who has lost a spouse only to see him remarry or otherwise attach to someone else shortly after the funeral. Many grownchildren feel disappointed or angry, even disgusted, and it is not unusual for them to reprimand their parent as if he were a teenager for showing such poor judgment. "Don't you feel any sadness for losing Mom?" and, "How could you be so disloyal to Mom?" are common reactions. Other grownchildren consider such hasty replacements as a blessing because it relieves the parent's loneliness and, at the same time, relieves them of additional burdens.

Here is a story told to us by grownchildren distressed at the behavior of their father, Saul, after their mother's death.

◆

Mom always treated Dad royally. He demanded it, and she, a dutiful and loving wife, went along willingly. When she died, his principal reaction was not sorrow or grief but concern over how his needs would be taken care of. He expected us to devote ourselves to him completely regardless of the inconvenience, insisting that one of us come to his house whenever he wanted, cook for him, and take him everywhere.

We gave him as much time as we could, and he continued to vent his anger whenever we didn't live up to his expectations. After a few months of this, Dad met Eleanor, an attractive woman who had lost her husband a while earlier, and they were soon married. On the one hand, this was a relief. But on the other hand, when we heard that Eleanor's husband had waited on her all their married life just as Mom had waited on Dad, we worried about the match. And, boy, were we right!

Just as Dad expected Eleanor to replace Mom, Eleanor expected him to replace her first husband. And, of course, neither did. Dad was disappointed in this turn of events, but he still considered it a feather in his cap to have won over this attractive widow, a trophy of sorts among his friends at the country club. Since his new wife didn't cook, they would continue to have dinner at one of our homes, or have one of us bring over whatever we'd made for their dinner. He expected us to transport both of them wherever they wanted, even though he could well afford taxis. If one of us was a little late with a phone call, he would become sarcastic and comment, "So what can I expect from a daughter who is too busy to phone?" or fly into a rage with, "After all I've done for you, don't I deserve more than this!"

◆

We explained that their father's failure to grieve didn't mean he didn't love their mother. He was just at a loss without her love, attention, and constant adoration.

◆

When your parent replaces a spouse, it means he can't get along alone.

If you are in a similar situation, you will find it relieving once you come to accept that regardless of what you think, your parent will do what he wants to do for better or worse. So let go of your need to stop him.

Accept your parent's right to make his own choices, for better or worse.

One of the reasons you are bound to be so upset is that you feel at the command of your parent's demanding behavior, and you feel guilty about saying "no." For your own well being, you have to do something about that guilt, and you have to take charge and decide for yourself what you can reasonably do for him.

If your parent is like Saul, you know this is easier said than done. In the midst of your own grief for your mother, you are prone to overdo for

◆

Decide what you can reasonably do.

your father and slip right into the role of "mate" before you recognize what is happening. It is important for you to try to be objective. It might even be helpful to sit down and compose a chart similar to the following, listing the ways you can help your parent and preserve yourself at the same time. The act of writing this list will help you impose objectivity on the situation.

MY REASONABLE "DO" LIST FOR DAD

- ◆ Grocery shop once a week, along with a two-hour visit.
- ◆ Talk on the phone every Tuesday and Thursday night.
- ◆ Be on call in real emergencies.
- ◆ Be in touch with his doctors if necessary.
- ◆ See that transportation is provided to doctor's appointments.

Survivors of Trauma May Find It Hard to Grieve

◆

Learn whatever you can about your parent's past. You may be able to use some of the specifics to help both of you in the mourning process.

Long-term reactions to serious traumas are not uncommon—they are often diagnosed as post-traumatic stress disorder. PTSD victims carry the emotional scars of their experiences throughout their lives. Since loss is an inseparable part of these experiences, victims have a difficult time mourning their losses and moving on. If your parent has been traumatized in this way and if he is making himself and you miserable, follow our guidelines to break through the angry no-win impasse between the two of you. The first step is to pay attention to the source of your parent's abuse and try to understand what he must be going through.

The most usual source of PTSD is physical or sexual abuse in childhood. The child suffers not only from the abuse itself but also from the feeling of having been let down by one or both of his parents or other family member. More often than not the victims blame themselves, believing they must have done something to cause the abuse. A chronic self-esteem problem plagues these individuals, who go through life expecting bad treatment from others.

PTSD is often found in the victims of other kinds of traumatic events—for example, it is common among battlefield veterans. Survivors of the Holocaust often suffer from the disorder and are probably the most studied victims of catastrophic trauma. They may have defended themselves against their memories of loss by plunging themselves vigorously into their work or other activities. Now, in later life, when they are no longer capable of such vigorous activity, disturbing flashbacks are more likely to occur that threaten their very core. Here is a story about one such survivor whose experiences in Nazi Germany have haunted him all his life. Although the story is about a particular survivor, his attitudes and behavior are typical not only of other survivors but of victims of trauma from other sources.

◆

Shortly after Hitler came to power, Otto's parents were imprisoned. He and his sister ran from place to place within Germany until they were finally able to leave the country for Italy. It seemed at first like a fortunate choice. Italy was hospitable, and the refugees managed to live there reasonably well. It was there he met and married Martha, another German refugee. Then Italy and Germany forged an alliance, which forced all the German refugees to flee. Martha and Hugo ran from country to country, finally reaching New York just before the war broke out. After the war they settled in Los Angeles, where Hugo established a successful business and they raised a family.

Neither Hugo nor Martha would ever say much about their experiences in Europe. All Hugo would talk about was what a bad decision he had made in choosing Italy as the place to go. His daughter, Harriet, recalled that her father always had trouble making decisions. He would always use the expression "Don't leave yourself sitting between two chairs" when Hugo would advise her about decisions to be made. It meant never make a move without knowing that you had a better place awaiting you. Hugo always acted according to that principle.

Martha made all the decisions throughout their married life. Then Martha died. In the days following the funeral, Hugo said little about his wife. He did not even seem particularly sad at her loss. He was entirely focused on where he should move. He knew all the living options and discussed them thoroughly with his children. But he couldn't make the decision and follow through on it. Over and over he would make a choice, put down a deposit, and then get cold feet, feeling as though he had made the worst mistake of his life. As Harriet said when she came to us for help, "It's as if my father is frozen to the floor."

◆

Hugo's indecisiveness was connected with the anguish he felt over his multiple experiences with moves in his earlier years. Decisions for Hugo had life-and-death consequences, especially those involved with going from place to place. He was indeed tied to his chair, repetitively reexperiencing his history and unable to move on.

Hugo's inability to make decisions was perhaps unique to the particular circumstances of his life. He tried to avoid his grief over the loss of his dear wife by moving on to a safer place. Yet he couldn't follow through for fear that the next place might bring further loss and further grief. This inability to grieve is something shared by many survivors of the Holocaust, and, indeed, of survivors of other kinds of traumatic experiences.

Of course, Hugo is only one survivor of Hitler's Holocaust. His experience left him with a particular set of psychological scars. Other Holocaust survivors, especially those who were imprisoned in the death camps, have different psychological scars. Yet they share a common difficulty in mourning because the losses of the present bring back memories and emotions that they have been trying to forget. To mourn these losses and accept the premeditated murder of millions of people is, for some, a kind of acquiescence that it was justified. For some there is guilt that they survived and so many others did not. For others there is a feeling they were abandoned by God and man.

Many try to erase the past—cut it off, amputate it, so to speak. But try as they might, survivors cannot forget this past. As Elie Wiesel says of himself and his fellow survivors, "We don't live in the past; the past lives in us." Thus as survivors try like everyone else to sum up their lives in old age, reliving their experiences often leaves them feeling dehumanized. For example, it is common for survivors to treat institutionalization in a nursing home as incarceration in a camp. The son of one such client could no longer care for his mother at home, yet he could not bring himself to move her into the nursing home nearby where she would get the needed round-the-clock medical care. From past experiences with his mother, he was afraid this would bring back concentration camp memories for her. But each person experiences life in his own unique way. We used information his mother had shared with us about having spent some of the war years in a convent where the nuns had treated her with loving care. When we introduced the need for a nursing home, we encouraged her to reflect back to the nunnery, where she'd learned to sew and knit and where she'd felt so loved and secure. These images allowed her to make the transition and an excellent adjustment to the home.

Helping People Mourn with Therapy and Related Programs

Common to all the people in the preceding examples was an inability to mourn the losses of their later years in normal ways. Each for his or her own special reason could not face up to the events of their earlier years and therefore could not go through the healthy summation process described by authors such as Erik Erikson and Judith Viorst, to whom we referred at the beginning of the chapter. In each situation the parent's difficulty with his or her losses was painful both to the parents and their children.

These are all people who need specialized help in the mourning process, and the following pages discuss some of the ways they can be helped. As we have seen earlier, many people resist therapy. Our emphasis, therefore, is just as much on how to introduce this special help in nonthreatening ways as on the specific therapies.

Even in the later years your parents can benefit from new insights through counseling. The one-on-one attention of a therapist may offer just the right amount of emotional support to help

◆

Therapy helps people mourn, no matter how old they are.

tide a person over in a crisis. Some parents, even those who may have resisted therapy all their lives, may be receptive at the time of crisis.

◆

Even a resistant parent
may be open to
therapy for specific
practical purposes.

Even people who believe that "counseling is for crazy people and I'm not crazy" may accept counseling focused on specific tasks and couched in acceptable terms. For example, a person such as Hugo, who would never hear of therapy all his life, might accept *relocation counseling* to help him solve the dilemma over moving, or *adjustment counseling* to help him in his first months of living in a senior residence. Similarly, a parent who has just lost a spouse might accept the idea of *bereavement counseling* or, if that is too much, of simply talking to someone about his sleepless nights.

◆

Find a geriatric
counselor who will
come to your parent's
house.

Some geriatric therapists make home visits. A parent with all kinds of excuses for not visiting a counselor may find it less intimidating having the therapist come to his home, where he can feel more in control.

◆

Anticipatory grieving is
very helpful.

Here are some other specialized forms of counseling that can be very helpful in times of loss: Especially effective is counseling prior to the death of the spouse or another loved one. In those instances, when the death process is slow, this can provide an opportunity for a parent to talk about what they are going through. The process of counseling can help the parent share some of their negative and angry feelings. The aim is to lead the parent to a greater degree of acceptance of this anger and to free up the more loving feelings.

It may be that your parent will see a counselor only if you go together. If you are in this position, by all means go. It will help you as well as your parent.

◆

Get your parent to a
doctor for medication
evaluation and therapy.

Especially in times of crisis, medications can be extremely effective in fighting anxiety and depression. The ideal way to do this is for your parent to see a geriatric psychiatrist for an evaluation for psychotropic medications and then for follow-up visits. What if your parent resists because she is frightened of being crazy? One way we have found to be effective is to avoid or deemphasize the use of the word "psychiatrist." Introduce the doctor as a "specialist" who will help with the right medication for sleeping, nervousness, or whatever form the major complaint takes. If the parent still resists, try going through the person's family doctor. He may consult with a geriatric psychiatrist on appropriate medication.

If your parent refuses even this, maybe someone else can be more successful than you in reaching your parent—perhaps a close friend or relative, a minister, or a trusted lawyer or accountant. You might also try writing your concerns down in a letter to your

◆

Don't force the issue unless you think your parent's health is at risk.

parent, a technique that we described in Chapter 7. If everything fails, there is no choice but to tell yourself you have done your best and give up—but only temporarily. Try again some time later. Only if you think your parent's health is at risk should you be more insistent. (See Chapter 3 for some examples of extreme risk.) If you are unsure of how to weigh the risks, consult with a mental health professional about your concerns.

Family therapy. Therapy sessions with family members can improve the communication between parents and children to the benefit of both. This kind of therapy is especially helpful for Holocaust survivors and their children. Another benefit is to help you maintain a relationship with your parent without either becoming overinvolved or, at the other extreme, cutting off. But don't be surprised or disappointed if your parent refuses to participate. If so, you might start by going with the rest of the family or by yourself, leaving it open for your parent to join you for later sessions.

Group therapy. A parent who is unwilling to go for therapy either alone or together with family members may be willing to join a group of others in similar circumstances. Therapy groups are led by trained professionals for treatment of psychological problems.

Support groups. Many people find bereavement or other support groups to be very helpful at times of loss. These groups may or may not be led by a professional and may be peer groups without a leader. The goals are more oriented to encouragement and support rather than psychological change as with the previous category, group therapy. Support groups for Holocaust survivors and their families have proven to work particularly well. The goals of these latter groups are both to help the older survivors find meaning in their own lives and to interrupt the transmission of their problems to the next generation. Such groups, sponsored by community social service organizations, have been of great assistance to many people.

Therapeutic programs. Conventional therapy, whether individual, family, or in groups, is not for everyone. Some people actually feel worse after reminiscing about their past because it stirs up such painful feelings as guilt, sadness, or rejection, which spirals them downward. In these situations, the therapy might be a meaningful activity or program that engages the parent in a more immediately uplifting way. For example, participation in the activities at senior nutrition sites, senior centers, YMCAs, and community centers can be very helpful to seniors. Social groups sponsored by churches and synagogues offer varied activities, including volunteer work, which can be the best therapy for some people. Call the Eldercare Locator number at 1-800-677-1116.

Some individuals respond better one-on-one rather than in a group. Be aware of this when planning a program. One client said his best therapy was engaging him in a volunteer program of visiting homebound people. In another situation, we arranged a weekly checkers game held in the client's home.

Keep in mind that there is a whole array of alternative therapies that may be preferable to conventional talking therapy for some people. Some examples are *art therapy, behavioral modification, movement therapy,* and *massage therapy.* These can be arranged one-on-one under the supervision of trained professionals.

In the end, your parent may not be receptive to any of

these therapeutic approaches. If so, pay special attention to all the things in the earlier part of the chapter that you yourself can do to cope with a parent whose past keeps him from facing his losses.

The Summation Process of Later Life

We conclude this chapter as we began, with Judith Viorst's words: "The people we are and the lives that we lead are determined, for better or worse, by our loss experiences."

In reading this chapter, you have seen examples of older people whose personalities prevent them from facing their losses, mourning them appropriately, and then moving on with their lives. Always remember that any kind of loss, separation, or change is very difficult for people whose behaviors reflect abandonment in the early years or a prior catastrophic trauma. This is when all their old issues will surface and their difficult behaviors will become most exaggerated. Simply understanding this will help you if only to keep you from doing and saying things that make the situation worse.

Do as much as your parent allows in helping him come to terms with his losses in the summing-up process of later life. Don't get too discouraged and frustrated when your parent does not respond as much as you would like. It may just be beyond his ability to meet your expectations. Always keep in mind it's not an all-or-nothing situation. Even a little movement toward appropriate mourning is better than nothing. And even if you have to settle for not making things worse, try to think of yourself as being guided by the physician's dictum that has stood the test of time: "Do no harm."

9

HOW TO KEEP FROM BEING DIFFICULT YOURSELF

Up to now, this book has been about helping grownchildren cope with their difficult older parents. Each of the preceding chapters has stressed the two aspects of this theme: First, understand why your parent behaves as she does; and second, use this understanding to improve the way you interact with your parent. All the many tips in the book are to this end.

If you have read these chapters and have taken the advice to heart, you have been able to change the way you interact with your parent and establish a *modus vivendi* that has been beneficial to both of you. You have probably also discovered that this same advice about understanding and dealing with your parent holds true when it comes to understanding and dealing with other people, for example, your relatives, your friends, your coworkers, your children, your spouse, indeed, everyone with whom you come into contact. For many of you this new insight is enough. But some of you may find this new way of dealing with your parent is giving you a view of *yourself* that you never had before. If so, you may find it profitable to go a little further.

Your new insight may prompt you to ask yourself, "Am *I*, sometimes, a little overly critical, negative, or controlling toward my spouse and children and coworkers? In short, am I behaving toward others just a little like my difficult parent has been behaving toward me?" If so, you may wonder whether you have perhaps inherited your parent's ways or have been influenced by your upbringing to behave like your parent. Perhaps you worry that with these tendencies you now see in yourself you will become more like your parent as you age—that you will become more rigid and unable to adapt to growing old, and that you will be dominated by your worst personality traits. Finally, you may be concerned that in the future your children will be in the same pickle with you as you are with your parent today.

But remember there is a major difference between you and your parent: You have read this book and have gained an awareness of your behavioral reactions that your parent never gained. And with this awareness, you have the opportunity to change your behavior. The way you have been up to now is a product of your genes, your upbringing, and your life experiences. But remember that your life experiences now include your newfound self-awareness. Once you recognize this, you have taken the first basic step toward doing something about the way you behave. It is now within your control to age without being difficult like your parent. With a willingness to look at yourself and the motivation to change the patterns that don't work, you can stop worrying that your children will be buying this book to learn how to cope with you.

A Daughter Recognizes That She Is Like Her Mother

For an example of the power of new insight, let's go back to the two sisters, Susan and Betsy, whom we met in the case study at the beginning of Chapter 5. From childhood on, these two women were held in tight check by a controlling mother. Susan was so bothered by this control that she sought the help of a counselor, who gave her the support she needed when she attempted to loosen her mother's grip by calling her three times a week instead of every day. As you recall, this mother was unable to accept this challenge to her authority and she cut her daughter off entirely. Moreover, she forced her husband and her other daughter, Betsy, to do the same.

With the support of the counselor, Susan had the strength to hold her ground while enduring the painful loss of her parents and sister. Betsy, in contrast, remained in her mother's orbit and began to treat her own children as her mother treated her. It was only many years later that Susan came to us after a worn-out Betsy had reconnected with her for help with her sick and aging parents. Betsy not only got some needed help from her sister in dealing with their parent's aging problems, but was forced to reexamine the big family break that had occurred so many years earlier. Here is a part of the conversation between the two sisters.

BETSY: When I think back to that time when you had your big fight with Mom, I feel very guilty. You know, Mom had me brainwashed. She had me believing you were the bad daughter who left us all. I always thought of myself as the dutiful daughter who stayed close to Mom and Dad. I just didn't have the willpower to resist Mom. How did you get the courage to do this?

SUSAN: It wasn't so much courage as it was necessity. I just got to the point where I couldn't stand calling Mom every day, when I had nothing to say, simply because she insisted on it. It was making me sick. I would start each day being disagreeable with Stan at breakfast and with my coworkers at the office until I got the phone call to Mom over with. I just couldn't stand it anymore. I knew the repercussions would be tremendous. I knew Mom might never speak to me again. But I had Stan by my side. He insisted I do something to break the unhealthy ties. And I knew Stan was right on, that the telephone problem was just one example of the unhealthy connection between us.

I began seeing a therapist, and she helped a lot. She helped me realize that while I was still young I had no choice but to remain under Mom's controlling thumb. It was the only way I still could have her mothering me the best she knew how. But the therapist showed me that now

I was a grown woman with a family of my own, I didn't need that kind of mothering anymore.

This conversation opened Betsy's eyes. Not only did she begin to understand her sister for the first time, but she began to look at herself in a new way. Was she, in fact, holding on to her own children as her mother was holding on to her? She didn't want to end up like her mother—bitter and cut off from her own children.

Perhaps you see a little of Betsy in yourself. If so, read on and see how you can take a closer look at your own behavior patterns.

An Attitude Shift

A good place to start is to examine in some detail how you behave in reaction to your difficult parent. What do you do when she drives you up the wall? Do you withdraw, blow a fuse, want to cut off, act in passive-aggressive, punitive, or manipulative ways? In other words, do you behave in ways similar to those of the difficult parents in the earlier chapters?

Sometimes it is hard to remember exactly how you react— it is so easy to forget the way you dealt with your parent yesterday. For this reason, it is helpful to keep a log of your reactions to your parent. Remember Al, the grownchild in Chapter 1 who became infuriated at his mother, Bea, who hung up on him when he called from the theater a little too late for her. We urged Al to keep such a log. On one side of the page he listed the comments his mother made that triggered his strong reactions. On the other side, he listed what particular emotions he felt in response to those comments. Here is his log *before* he got professional help.

WHEN MY MOTHER SAYS:	I FEEL:
"Where were you?"	furious.
nothing, just hangs up on me	pained, rejected, cut off.
"You don't care about me"	guilty.

Note how some of these reactions are similar to his mother's. Al is *personalizing*. He feels more like a little boy who has been chastised than a grown man. His mother's comments get under his skin just as they did when he was living under his parents' roof as a child. His feelings of guilt and fury are a knee-jerk response, very automatic and ingrained over many years. And like many grownchildren, Al feels deeply responsible for his mother's unhappiness. At times he even considers changing jobs to have more time with her. Other times, he never wants to see her again. Al needs perspective. He is caught in an emotional mire—entangled with his mother in a way that doesn't afford him an adult relationship with her. What helped him gain more perspective was committing to writing an "objective profile" of his mother, Bea.

MY OBJECTIVE PROFILE OF BEA

My mother is overly dependent on me. The assaults she hurls at me are not rational. I think this is due to hardships she endured in her early life—her mother's preoccupation with her sick child followed by years of depression. Without an attentive mother, my mother never learned a sense of self-acceptance. She could not stand on her own two feet or allow me to become self-sufficient as I was growing up. She always needed the emotional security of someone else: first her own mother, then my father, and now me. She never learned to drive, write checks, or, for that matter, let me go to a college away from home. She never developed normal coping tools.

Al's profile of his mother helped him stay on track. For example, when he found himself spending much more time with his mother out of guilt than with his wife and children, he recalled this objective profile. He was then able to balance his time in a way that made sense to him and accept his mother's disappointment. But he no longer feels as responsible or guilty about this decision. Instead, he recognizes his mother's limitations, rather than trying to make up for them.

With professional help, Al became less reactive and more at peace within himself about how he was coping with his mother. Although his mother's behavior is the same, his side of the log now looks quite different.

WHEN MY MOTHER SAYS:	I FEEL:
"Where were you?"	compassion, sympathy.
nothing, just hangs up	momentarily angry.
"You don't care about me"	sad for her.

Curiously, Al now feels sad when he thinks about his mother. As he gives up the notion of trying to make his mother happier, his most significant reaction is a surprising one—a sense of loss and of mourning. What is this all about?

Mourning a Living Parent

In Chapter 8 we saw that successful mourning means coming to terms with a loss over time and then moving on with one's life. In contrast, mourning is unsuccessful when the person is unable to come to terms with the loss for any of a variety of reasons.

The story of Susan and Betsy that we referred to earlier gives us a graphic example of mourning a living parent. Susan's mother cut her off completely and, at the same time, forced her husband and her other daughter, Betsy, to do the same. Susan was, therefore, confronted with the loss of both parents and a sister in one blow. Although the loss of her closest family members in this way was devastating, with the help of the counselor she was able to confront the losses and mourn them appropriately.

Al's losses are less severe and less obvious than Susan's. What he lost was his unrealistic image of his mother. With newfound insight into his mother's personality, he was able to face the reality that his mother only had the capacity to take from him and no capacity to give to him, no matter what he did. In short, he recognized she wasn't and never would be the parent he wished for. Giving up the hope that your parent will one day show you more acceptance and love is an extremely painful experience. One son described it aptly when he said that it made him feel like someone orphaned at birth who had never had a real mother.

Al knew he had to reduce his almost daily visits with his mother for the sake of his marriage and health. From his counseling sessions he knew this would bring out his mother's feelings of desertion and that she would blame him. He was less prepared for his own reaction. On the one hand, he was relieved he had less contact with her. But along with this was a feeling of sadness when his mother chastised him for not being "a good son."

These are all losses that can be dealt with. As Al comes to accept his mother with her limitations, he has a double reward. Not only will he ease the burdens and stresses that the relationship with his mother has placed on him, but he will be better prepared for his own aging. Recall how in the last chapter we described old age as the time when we look back on our lives and come to terms with it. The greater our capacity to mourn our losses, the more satisfactory is this summation process. Thus the greater Al's capacity to mourn his losses now when he is middle-aged, the better prepared he will be later when he is older and the losses multiply in number and severity. Not only will he interact more satisfactorily with his wife and children and others around him, but his own aging process will be more successful. He will be serving as a model for his children and later generations.

Remember the difficulty some of the people in the case studies of the last chapter had in mourning their losses? Fortunately for Al, his personality mimicked his mother's to only a small degree, and he has had a relatively easy time mourning his losses. How about Betsy, whose personality appeared to be a carbon copy of her mother's? Recall that she reconnected with her sister Susan only to obtain some relief from the care of her sick mother and father. But Susan and our counselor gave Betsy more than she asked for. For the first time Betsy understood what her sister had gone through and why she'd had to do what she had done. For the first time she had an inkling of her mother's personality and the relationship between her mother and herself. And, most importantly, for the first time Betsy took a look inside herself. For Betsy to change significantly after all these years would take more counseling than Al had required. But once she understood what was to be gained for herself, her husband, and her children, she was willing to undertake the counseling route.

When Your Difficult Parent Dies

It is always hard to lose a parent. It is especially hard when you lose a parent toward whom you have had negative or ambivalent feelings. Mourning such a parent is much more complex than mourning a parent with whom you had a loving and positive relationship. There is a profound sense of sadness and loss about something you never had. There is no longer the chance to improve the relationship and to win acceptance and love. Many grownchildren who have come for counseling over the death of a difficult parent have told us that their sadness is mostly over the lost opportunities. When your parent dies it is all over. There is no more time to heal a breach or improve a bad relationship.

Often the grownchildren of difficult parents experience relief when the difficult parent dies. These grownchildren typically find themselves at the funeral with little or no feeling for the parent, only a profound sense that it is over. This feeling of relief is a natural reaction to all the pain and disappointment they have felt over their lifetimes. Put yourself in the place of such a grownchild. You may have been a caregiver for the last months or years of your parent's life. You may have had to sacrifice your personal time attending a parent who may not have done a good job of attending to you while you were growing up. All the resentment of caring for an ailing parent who is not appreciative or has a poor track record in raising you may dissolve into relief when your parent dies. You are glad to be free of your burden. You can't feel love, and anger is out of place. Your immediate reaction may be to feel nothing.

You may think you can now start to recuperate, like this son who said, "After Dad died, I realized I was totally worn out from the years of worry and care. I'm depleted and I need to recuperate almost like I've had a long illness myself." Others may believe they've already done their mourning, as, for example, the woman who told us, "I feel a lot of relief and some sadness over my mother's death. I already did a lot of grieving over what we didn't have together."

Although relief is a natural reaction at first, be aware there may be other feelings that need expression. It may be relieving to close the book and move on. We encourage you to keep it open and be prepared for any feelings that may yet surface. For some people, anger is the overriding and safer feeling, and it serves to keep hidden any loving memories. Others may idealize a parent and feel guilty whenever negative reminders emerge. Successful mourning requires a balanced view. The more you are aware of your mixed feelings about your parent, the less susceptible you are to having the problems spill over into your everyday life and be replayed in your current interactions. For instance, you may fight with your siblings, trying to get from them what you wanted from your parents. Or you might provoke your boss just as you did your parent, without realizing you are merely repeating a pattern.

The good news is that with the end of this chapter of your life, you now have a further opportunity for self-growth and freedom. Whether or not you started the grieving process before your parent died, you can now continue onward. One client said, "After Mom died, I realized how much of myself was given over to please her, boost her self-esteem. Now I can start to discover all that I am and start giving to myself."

For some, this freedom to explore different directions is anxiety provoking. Even though your parent is no longer placing demands on your time and energy, you may still feel uneasy. The reality is that you have lost the role of being a grownchild or caregiver to your difficult parent. And as with any loss, this role change can bring a sense of uncertainty.

If you feel stuck and can't seem to move along with your mourning, grief therapy can be very useful. One client, Janet, came to us for therapy while her overcritical mother was dying of cancer. She longed for her mother to understand her better and be more affectionate. During the course of her therapy, she was able to take a close look at her mother's rocky beginnings and resulting low self-esteem. This enabled her to begin her own grieving process over her profound disappointment that from her earliest years her mother could never be the kind of mother she had needed. At the funeral, she was able to focus on some of her mother's strengths and wasn't consumed by her negative feelings. This anticipatory grief counseling helped her move on with her life.

You should think of the period of time immediately following your parent's death as a time of transition, a time to explore a direction that is right for you. Grief therapy worked well for Janet. Other clients have done other things that were helpful in making the transition. Here are some of them.

renewed old friendships

did volunteer work

reprioritized their work and personal time

undertook a program of exercise and diet

returned to earlier hobbies and interests

caught up on their reading and took vacations

just did nothing as a way of regrouping

Allowing yourself a time of transition and labeling it as such is a good idea. You need time to grieve and renew yourself.

A Final Word

The first step in keeping from being difficult yourself is to be open to examining your own behavior. If you are receiving negative feedback from colleagues, friends, and family, then that is a red flag for you. Go back and examine how you interacted with your parent, just as Al did after his mother's latest provocation, and as Betsy finally did after so many years of allowing herself to be controlled by her mother.

If you find some of your difficult parent in yourself, don't think you are doomed to age as she has aged. You have the ability to do something about it. You have the opportunity to change. It may not be easy, but persevere. The rewards are great.

PERSONALITY DISORDERS

The word *disorder* is used by physicians to describe categories of medical problems. Just as physical disorders—respiratory disorders, for example—are described by physical symptoms, emotional disorders are described by behavioral symptoms. Among the many kinds of emotional disorders is a category called *personality disorders.* The psychiatric diagnostic manual, *Diagnostic and Statistical Manual of Mental Disorders (DSM IV),* identifies ten such personality disorders, each characterized by a set of behaviors. A person is diagnosed with the disorder if he or she has some number of these behaviors— the ones in the questionnaire on page 2 are the ways we observe them in older people. Even though personality disorders are in the psychiatric category, it would be a mistake to say that those with personality disorders are necessarily "mentally ill." Rather, they have lifelong personality traits that set them apart and distress those around them.

There is a large body of professional literature on personality disorders written primarily by psychiatrists who treat people suffering from these disorders. Since older people almost never seek treatment for such disorders, the patients discussed in the professional literature are young to middle-aged. With psychotherapy, some of these younger people are able to come to terms with the underlying causes of their symptoms and go on to live more satisfying lives. However, most people with these symptoms do not undergo psychotherapy. Many manage to get by with supportive family members, especially spouses. Then later in life when they develop ailments and when their spouses take ill or die, the behaviors become more exaggerated, and their children come to us and other social workers for help in coping with their difficult parent.

When we learn about a parent's behaviors and background, we may conclude that she has a personality disorder. The main value of the diagnosis is to help a grownchild understand what is bothering his parent. With this understanding he may be able to modify his own behavior toward her by avoiding those things that trigger her worst behaviors and doing things that help her. Understanding that she is not deliberately trying to make his life miserable but has a problem as real as a physical problem may also help him develop more sympathy for her.

Types of Personality Disorders

Of the ten personality disorders, two are especially common. In the lead is the *borderline personality disorder,* and behind it is the *narcissistic personality disorder.* In most cases, the name gives us a clue as to what the disorder is about. For example, the term *narcissism* is commonly used in everyday conversation, so we have some understanding, simply from the name, of how people with this disorder behave. This is not true for the borderline personality. Its name is an unfortunate accident of history, conceived decades ago when little was known about it. Although much more has been learned in the years that have followed, the name remains.

In the common vernacular, a narcissistic person is someone with an overinflated opinion of himself—seemingly a person with very high self-esteem. But the paradox is that a person with the narcissistic personality disorder has such low self-esteem that he needs the constant boosting of others to shore him up. The entries in the self-centered and control categories in the questionnaire are the principal ways in which he does this.

The borderline person appears to be the polar opposite of the narcissist. While the narcissist seems to be on top of the world, the borderline seems to be on the bottom: Like the narcissist, the borderline has low self-esteem, but, unlike the narcissist, the borderline's low self-esteem is usually evident to his children. A lack of identity or "self" is another way in which this low self-esteem is sometimes described, and the clinging behaviors in the dependency category in the questionnaire best reflect this characteristic. Still another behavior typical of the borderline is his propensity to *split* or turn hot and cold on those around him, for example, being unable to find anything bad about a grownchild on one day and anything good on the next. The borderline can, in fact, have any of the behaviors in the questionnaire. Of course, the most disturbing of these is self-abuse with the attendant risk of suicide.

It is understandable that an emotional disorder does not always have an obvious source as does a physical disorder such as diabetes. Still, researchers have seen enough examples of people with the borderline and narcissistic personality disorders to develop possible theories about their origins.

The Separation Theory

This brief discussion of the nature of the borderline and narcissistic personality disorders indicates that there is some similarity between the two, despite their external differences. The most widely held theory holds that both arise from feelings of abandonment originating in childhood. According to this theory something happens in a child's earliest years that prevents a normal separation from the mother. If you have observed the growing-up process in either your own or someone else's children, you recognize that within a few months of birth a child begins the long, gradual process of becoming an independent person in his own right. Beginning to walk near the first birthday is a step in the process of separating from the mother. The negative behavior of a two-year-old is a good illustration of a child struggling to assert a higher level of separateness and independence.

All babies struggle with this process of separating from their mothers. For example, a baby under one year old feels such close emotional ties to his mother that little acts of separation, such as the mother leaving the room, can leave him panicked that his mother will never return. Most children eventually resolve the problems of acquiring independence. But there are others who never succeed in doing this in a healthy way.

It may be the child—perhaps because of his genetic makeup—whose attachment to the mother makes it difficult for him to separate normally. It may also be the mother who impedes the normal separation process, either by a smothering dependency of her own that keeps her from letting the child exercise independence, or a premature separation beyond her control, for example, by an illness that forces her to leave the baby in someone else's care.

The consequence of the child's failure to separate adequately, usually in the first three years, is a depression that theorists call the *abandonment depression*. A baby whose connection to his mother is damaged continues to suffer the emotional pain of this depression during the remainder of his childhood and into adulthood. This is in contrast to a baby who separates normally in her earliest years and is able to continue the process of emotional growth as she grows up physically. So devastating are these feelings of abandonment that the child unconsciously develops emotional safeguards known as *defense* or *coping* mechanisms that relieve the depression. The behaviors listed in the questionnaire are the way these coping mechanisms show up. Combinations of these behaviors are typically associated with borderline and narcissistic personalities. For example, a narcissistic person whose self-centered behaviors continually remind her children of how wonderful she is may really be covering a deep feeling of depression stemming from a perceived early rejection by her mother. Another person might handle the same feelings by being hostile to her children whenever they fail to treat her as she thinks they should.

The separation theory provides a plausible explanation of splitting, the black-and-white behavior so characteristic of the borderline personality disorder. Every child has ambivalent feelings toward his mother in the separation process. On the one hand, he is striving for independence, but at the same time, the toddler is careful not to stray too far away, always watching to be sure his mother is there. In a baby's primitive view, his mother is split into two people: a "bad," depriving mother from whom he is seeking more independence, and a "good," nurturing mother who is always there if he should need support and comfort as he widens his horizons.

In normal development, a child fuses together the "good" and the "bad" mother images in the early years so that he eventually accepts his mother as an integrated human being with strengths and weaknesses. He continues this process of separation from his mother throughout childhood and adolescence. In contrast, the child with separation problems retains the dual images. He grows up with the emotional makeup of the toddler as he continues to seek comfort from his "good" mother to overcome the depression resulting from being abandoned by his "bad" mother. Instead of developing a mature understanding of his mother as a multifaceted human being as he grows older, he becomes stuck with the infantile response to separateness with its inability to resolve the split between the "good" and "bad" mothers.

Later in life, this person may transfer this love/hate relationship from his mother to a spouse, and, still later, to a grownchild. His split view of the world remains unless he undergoes a long enough term of psychotherapy to heal the split. As we pointed out earlier, the vast majority of people suffering with this personality disorder cannot or do not take this route, which is why we see so many people with borderline personalities in the older population.

The separation theory is a satisfying way of explaining the behavior of many of the troubled older people we have seen in our practice. When we are able to convince a grownchild that the fear of stirring up old abandonment feelings is what is driving his parent's behavior, then he will be cognizant of things he does that may trigger these fears and can try to avoid them. The grownchild who has come to realize that a parent with this personality suffers from being unable to control her extreme reactions when she anticipates a separation from those close to her will have come a long way in dealing with his mother's basic difficulties and in lessening his desperation.

The Abuse Theory

A second common theory attributes the borderline personality disorder to trauma from sexual or other abuse—the technical term is *post-traumatic stress disorder* (PTSD), which we referred to in Chapter 8. The theory relating borderline behavior to this disorder was developed in more recent years by therapists who observed that a substantial portion of their borderline patients reported abuse of some sort earlier in life. According to this theory, the person abused in early life keeps replaying the trauma unconsciously in later life. Knowledge of such early abuse can help the psychotherapist in treating these patients.

The victims of sexual, physical, or emotional abuse are left with psychic scars not only of the abuse itself but also of the feeling of having been let down by one or both of the parents. An abusing father not only deserts his child by abdicating his role as a protector, but the child feels unprotected and deserted by the mother as well. If someone other than the parent is the abuser, then, regardless of the circumstances, the child can feel unprotected and abandoned by both parents. Thus the fear of abandonment is also a powerful consequence of abuse as well as of separation difficulties. Because of this, the underlying abandonment theme is the most meaningful tool we have in our role with our client population of elders and their families.

If the grownchild knows enough of the parent's background to be aware of or suspect abuse, this knowledge can play a role in developing a more sympathetic reaction to a parent's trying behavior. However, all too often the grownchild hears little or nothing of the specifics from his parent, who has been trying all his life to suppress the horrors. In this common situation, the grownchild can only imagine what might have happened, and try to piece together information from other family sources.

BIBLIOGRAPHY

There are many books and articles that can be helpful to readers. We have divided them into the four categories that follow. The books in the first three categories are for the general reader; those in the fourth category are for professionals.

1. General books on aging

Billig, Nathan. *To Be Old and Sad—Understanding Depression in the Elderly,* Lexington Books, Lexington, MA, 1987.

Billig, Nathan. *Growing Older and Wiser,* Lexington Books, New York, 1993.

Butler, Robert N. *Why Survive? Being Old in America,* Harper and Row, New York, 1975.

Butler, Robert H. and Myrna Lewis. *Aging and Mental Health,* Merrill (MacMillan), New York, 1981.

Erikson, Erik H. "Identity and the Life Cycle," *Psychology Issues,* Vol 1, No. 1 (Monograph 1) International University Press, New York, 1959.

Friedan, Betty. *The Fountain of Age,* Simon & Schuster, New York, 1993.

Silverstone, Barbara and Hyman and Helen Kandel. *Growing Old Together,* Pantheon, New York, 1992.

Tobin, Sheldon S. *Personhood in Advanced Old Age,* Springer Publishing Co., New York, 1991.

Viorst, Judith. *Necessary Losses,* Random House, New York, 1996.

2. Books on eldercare

Bumagin, Victoria E. and Kathryn P. Hirn. *Aging is a Family Affair,* A Lippincott and Crowell Book, New York, 1979.

Cohen, Donna and Carl Eisdorfer. *Caring for Your Aging Parents,* G. Putnam and Sons, New York, 1993.

Cohen, Stephen Z. and Bruce M. Gans. *The Other Generation Gap: The Middle-Aged and Their Aging Parents.* New Century, Piscataway, NJ, 1978.

Edinberg, Mark A. *Talking With Your Aging Parents,* Shambhala, Boston, 1988.

Gottlieb, Daniel with Edward Claflin. *Family Matters: Healing in the Heart of the Family,* Dutton, New York, 1991.

Levin, Nora Jean, *How to Care for Your Parents: A Practical Guide to Eldercare,* W. W. Norton, New York, 1997.

Levy, Michael T. *Parenting Mom and Dad,* Prentice Hall, New York, 1991.

Manning, Doug. *When Love Gets Tough,* In-sight Books, Inc., Hereford, TX, 1983.

Morris, Virginia. *How to Care for Aging Parents,* Workman Publishing Co., New York, 1996.

Shulman, Bernard H. and Raeann Berman. *How to Survive Your Aging Parent,* Surrey Books, Inc., Chicago, 1988.

3. Books and articles on difficult behaviors

Feil, Naomi. *The Validation Breakthrough,* Health Professions Press, Inc., 1993.

Forward, Susan. *Toxic Parents,* Bantam Books, New York, 1989.

Kreisman, Jerold J. and Hal Straps. *I Hate You, Don't Leave Me: Understanding the Borderline Personality,* Avon Books, New York, 1989.

Mace, Nancy and Peter Rabins. *The 36-Hour Day: A Family Guide to Caring for Persons with Alzheimer's Disease,*

Related Dementing Illness, and Memory Loss in Later Life, The Johns Hopkins University Press, Baltimore, 1981.

Mailer, Norman. *Marilyn: A Biography*, Grosset and Dunlop, Inc., New York, 1973.

Miracle, Berniece Baker and Mona Rae. *My Sister Marilyn: A Memoir of Marilyn Monroe*, Algonquin Books of Chapel Hill, 1994.

Sass, Louis. "The Borderline Personality," *The New York Times*, Aug. 22, 1982.

Secunda, Victoria. *When You and Your Mother Can't Be Friends*, Bantam Doubleday Dell Publishing Group, Inc., New York, 1990.

Steinem, Gloria. *Marilyn*, New American Library, New York, 1986.

Turecki, Stanley and Leslie Tonner. *The Difficult Child*, Bantam Books, New York, 1985.

4. Professional books and journal articles

Blazer, Dan. *Emotional Problems in Later Life: Interventive Strategies for Professional Caregivers*, Springer Publishing Co., New York, 1990.

Clifton, Anne R. "Regression in the Search for a Self", *International Journal of Psychoanalytic Psychotherapy*, 1972.

Cohen, Norman A. "On Loneliness and the Ageing Process," *International Journal of Pyscho-Analysis*, vol 63, 149, 1982.

Danieli, Yael. "The Aging Survivor of the Holocaust Discussion: On the Achievement of Integration in Aging Survivors of the Nazi Holocaust," Presented at Boston Society for Gerontologic Psychiatry, Nov. 22, 1980.

Diagnostic and Statistical Manual of Mental Disorders (DSM-IV), American Psychiatric Association, Washington, 1996.

Freed, Anne. "The Borderline Personality," *Social Casework*, Nov. 1980.

Golomb, Elan. *Trapped in the Mirror: Adult Children of Narcissists in Their Struggle for Self,* William Morrow, New York, 1992.

Graziano, R. "Making the Most of your Time: Clinical Social Work With a Borderline Patient," *Clinical Social Work Journal,* 14 {3} Fall '86, p 262.

Griez, Roberta H. "Geriopsychiatric Partial Hospitalization Programs," Symposium of the Boston Society for Gerontologic Psychiatry, Inc., October 25, 1996.

Hobos, L. "The Borderline Patient: Theoretical and Treatment Considerations," *Clinical Social Work Journal,* 14 [1], '86, pp 66.

Kinsler, Florabel. "The Emotional and Physiological Issues of Aging in North American Holocaust Survivors: Implications for Other Refugee Populations, *GCM Journal,* Summer 1996.

Kroll, Jerome. *PTSD/Borderlines in Therapy,* W. W. Norton and Co., Inc., New York, 1993.

Lebow, Grace H. "Facilitating Adaptation in Anticipatory Mourning," *Social Casework,* July 1976.

Lebow, Grace H. and Barbara Kane. "The Assessment Function in Social Work Case Management," *Social Work Case Management,* edited by Betsy S. Vourlekis and Roberta R. Greene, Alaine De Gruyter, New York, 1992.

Levendusky, Phillip. "Cognitive Behavior Therapy as a Treatment for Depression in the Older Adult," Symposium of the Boston Society for Gerontologic Psychiatry, Inc., October 25, 1996.

Masterson, James F., M.D. *Psychotherapy of the Borderline Adult,* Brunner/Mazel, New York, 1976.

Masterson, James F., M.D. *The Search for the Real Self,* The Free Press, New York, 1988.

Pollock, George H. "On Aging and Psychopathology: Discussion of Dr. Norman A. Cohen's Paper 'On Loneliness and the Aging Process,' " *International Journal of Psycho-Analysis,* vol 63, 275, 1982.

Ruskin, Paul E. and John A. Talbot. *Aging and the Post-traumatic Stress Disorder,* American Psychiatric Press, Washington, 1996.

Sheikh, Jarvid, Ed. Irvin Yalom, General Ed., *Treating the Elderly,* Joffey-Bass, San Francisco, 1996.

Silver, Daniel and Michael Rosenbluth, Editors. *Handbook of Borderline Disorders,* International University Press, Madison, CN, 1992.

Simon, Robert I. *Bad Men Do What Good Men Dream,* American Psychiatric Press, Washington, 1996.

Steury, Steven and Marie L. Blank, Editors. *Readings in Psychotherapy with Older People,* U. S. Department of Health and Human Services, Alcohol, Drug Abuse, and Mental Health Administration, Rockville, MD, 1980.

Szabo, Peggy and Karen Boesch, "Impact of Personality and Personality Disorders in the Elderly," Chapter 5 of *Problem Behaviors in Long-Term Care,* Peggy Szabo and George T. Grossberg, Editors, Springer Publishing Co., Inc., New York, 1993.

Turner, Francis J., Editor. *Mental Health and the Elderly: A Social Work Perspective,* The Free Press, New York, 1992.

Vaillant, George E., M.D. "The Beginning of Wisdom is Never Calling a Patient a Borderline," *Jrn of Psychotherapy Practice and Research,* Vol 1, No 2, Spring 1992, pp 117–134.

Wolin, Steven J. and Sybil Wolin. *The Resilient Self: How Survivors of Troubled Families Rise above Adversity,* Villard Books, New York, 1994.

GRACE LEBOW, MSW, LCSW-C and BARBARA KANE, MSW, LCSW-C, the cofounders of Aging Network Services of Bethesda, Maryland, are clinical social workers and care managers, specializing in older people and their families. They created a nationwide network of similar professionals to work with geographically separated families. This is their first book.